About the author

Andrew Tomas, born in St. Petersburg in
1913 and now an Australian citizen, has
spent most of his life travelling extensively
throughout the world. In fact *Atlantis:
From Legend to Discovery* was begun in
Australia, continued in the Himalayas,
Russia and France and completed in
London. He is the author of the
bestselling book on the riddles of Ancient
Science, *We Are Not the First*.

*Also by Andrew Tomas and available
in Sphere Books*

WE ARE NOT THE FIRST

Atlantis:
From Legend to Discovery
ANDREW TOMAS

SPHERE BOOKS LIMITED
30/32 Gray's Inn Road, London WC1X 8JL

First published in Great Britain in 1972 by Robert Hale & Company
Copyright © Editions Robert Laffont 1972
First Sphere Books edition 1973
Reprinted September 1973
Reprinted October 1974

TRADE
MARK

Set in Linotype Lectura

Printed in Great Britain by
Hazell Watson & Viney Ltd
Aylesbury, Bucks

ISBN 0 7221 8542 1

CONTENTS

Dedicated to NICHOLAS ROERICH (1874–1947), artist, explorer and philosopher, who wrote this verse about a forgotten race:

> We do not know. But they know.
> The stones know,
> And they remember.
> Airships were flying.
> Came pouring a liquid fire.
> Came flashing
> The spark of life and death.
> By the might of spirit
> Stony masses ascended.
> Scriptures guarded wise secrets.
> And again all is revealed.

PREFACE

These lines are written on that illusive frontier which separates science from fantasy. Heinrich Schliemann walked on it with Homer's *Iliad* in his hand and found legendary Troy. Professor Hermann Oberth has confessed to the author that Jules Verne's *From the Earth to the Moon* prompted him to convert a romance into rocketry formulae. What is fiction today will be fact tomorrow.

The present work is intended to stir the interest of scientific circles and the public in general in one of the world's greatest riddles. Did Atlantis leave treasure vaults in or under the pyramids and the Sphinx as ancient tradition claims?

At the 1964 World's Fair in New York a time capsule was sunk into the ground with forty-four articles. Our predecessors in history could have done the same thing, leaving a bequest of priceless manuscripts and objects for future ages. In 1967 a joint United Arab Republic–United States of America 'Pyramid Project' was initiated to X-ray the pyramids with cosmic rays to determine the presence and location of secret crypts. A major archaeological discovery can be made in deep explorations at Gizeh.

In this era of unparalleled advancement of science it is timely to explore the unknown domains of knowledge in order to anticipate and even prompt discoveries yet to be made.

In his research the author has followed the precept of Galileo — "freely to question and freely to answer".

Once a youth stood before the image of Quetzalcoatl in Mexico City, reflecting upon the culture hero's links with legendary Atlantis.

In Los Angeles and Hollywood he frequented public libraries examining chronicles of the conquistadores and legends of the American Indians.

In Japan the man learned of a myth that formerly the earth had been connected with heaven by a bridge, and he thought of prehistoric space travel.

Taoists in China spoke to him about the abode of "immortals of the west" and Shambhala, the city of star-men.

In Australia he found out about Dreamtime, a forgotten epoch in which mankind commuted with the sky-beings.

Recently he beheld the mighty Kanchenjunga on Tibetan border, known as the Five Treasuries of the Great Snow, where secret treasures are believed to be stored from time immemorial.

In India he admired the Himalayas and listened to legends about the underground palaces and treasure-vaults of Nagas, the flying serpents who have brilliant lamps to illuminate their subterranean abodes.

The man lived in the Himalayan village of Manali which, according to Brahmin scriptures, was founded by Manu who had rescued his sages from the Great Flood in a bark.

Then he explored the Khufu Pyramid and asked the Sphinx for the answer to his age-old riddle.

In Austria he tried to solve the mystery of a polished steel cube found in a coal stratum, millions of years old.

At the Bibliotheque de l'Arsenal, near the Place de la Bastille in Paris, he perused eighteenth-century volumes of the 'Astronome du Roi' Jean-Sylvain Bailly. In the Louvre he found the ancient Egyptian Zodiac of Denderah.

Then he studied in the reading room of the British Museum

Library in London with its wealth of books and manuscripts of great antiquity.

After that—research work in the Lenin Library of Moscow, meetings with Russian scientists and writers, visits to the Hermitage Museum in Leningrad.

This tale is about the author of this book.

CHAPTER ONE

THE DOOM OF ATLANTIS

SEA AND VOLCANO AGAINST LAND

"The sky one second was intense blackness, and the next a blaze of fire. Such darkness and time of it in general few would conceive and many, I dare say, would disbelieve," wrote an eyewitness of the Krakatoa explosion in 1883.[1]

The island of Krakatoa, which is between Sumatra and Java, was blown away, creating a chasm on the sea bed. A 100-foot tidal wave hurled ships and boats onto hills. The echo of the eruption was heard as far as Australia and the atmosphere was disturbed all over the globe.

"The blinding fall of sand and stones, the intense blackness above and around us, broken only by the incessant glare of varied kinds of lightning and the continued explosive roars of Krakatoa, made our situation a truly awful one," recorded the seaman who saw the disaster.

One night in February 1966, I was aboard a liner passing through Sunda Strait. The weird glow of Krakatoa cast reddish lights on the sea and clouds. The fury of volcanic fires and tidal waves in the Krakatoa cataclysm suddenly rose before my eyes. But time will eventually obliterate the memory of this geological upheaval and only folk-tales will remember this dramatic incident of the past. Perhaps this is exactly what happened to the legendary Atlantis.

Are the continents permanent homes for the nations of today? Do the oceans remain in their beds forever? The answer is a brief no, with a long list of facts. Although history is far too short in terms of geological epochs, it has nevertheless recorded many marked geographical changes in the past.

The Etruscan city of Spina in the Adriatic, mentioned by Pliny the Elder and by Strabo, once a thriving metropolis of trade and culture, is now completely submerged. Dioscuria, the city in the Black Sea off Sukhumi visited by the legendary Argonauts, is at present under water. Phanagoria, an ancient Greek port of considerable size—also in the Black Sea—has sunk into the waters of Taman Bay.

Not only cities but huge land masses constantly disappear into the depths of the oceans as tectonic movements of the earth go on all the time. In this light, the sinking of Atlantis may be true. Land sinks and emerges from the sea floor in comparatively short periods of time. A review of these geological and geographical changes throughout the globe reveals surprising phenomena.

The temple of Jupiter-Serapis in the Bay of Naples was built in 105 B.C. It gradually sank into the Mediterranean, but in 1742 the temple rose again from the sea bottom. It is now sinking once more. The fortress of Caravan-Sarai in the Caspian Sea was erected in 1135. In the course of time it slowly disappeared under water. From then on all references to this fort in ancient records became so puzzling that Caravan-Sarai turned into a fable. In 1723 the islet rose above the sea and is still clearly visible.

Port Royal in Jamaica, a den of pirates, was badly shaken by an earthquake and partially submerged in 1692. In the Lisbon quake of 1755 the tidal wave was 33 feet high. Most of the city was destroyed and 60,000 residents lost their lives.

Falcon or Jack-in-the-Box Island was discovered in the South Pacific by Maurelle, a Spanish explorer, in 1780. The government of Tonga planted 2,000 coconut palms on the island in 1892, but two years later Falcon vanished under the surface of the ocean. It is coming up at present.

A violent earthquake shook the delta of the Indus in 1819. A vast territory was inundated and only the tallest buildings remained above water. Between 1822 and 1853 the coast of Chili rose by 30 feet as a result of severe earth tremors.

The Tuanaki in the Cook Islands sank in the Pacific Ocean with 13,000 inhabitants in the second half of the last century. One morning fishermen left the island in their boats. When they returned home at night, the island was gone.

A smoking mountain arose from the depths of the Atlantic

14

near the Azores in 1957. Also in the Azores, seven years later, an earthquake hit St George Island. The catastrophe was so serious that 15,000 residents had to leave the island. The volcano of Tristan da Cunha, thought to be extinct, erupted in the south Atlantic in 1961, bringing about the evacuation of its population to England.

Not only islands and coastlines but whole continents are either sinking or rising. France, for instance, is sinking at the rate of 30 centimetres a century. Land between the Ganges and the Himalayas is going up 18·1 millimetres per year. The Andes in South America are believed to have risen 200 to 300 feet since Columbus. The bottom of the Pacific Ocean is pushing toward the surface in the region of the Aleutian Islands. According to Father Joseph Lynch of Fordham University, New York, a new continent seems ready to rear its head above the surface of the Atlantic, too. This may be the Atlantis of myth and legend.

The scope of geological changes constantly taking place in the oceans is evident from a discovery made by the technicians of a Western Telegraph ship searching for a lost cable in the Atlantic Ocean in 1923. They detected that the cable had been thrown up by the rising ocean bed by $2\frac{1}{4}$ miles in only twenty-five years. If the Atlantic Ocean were to be suddenly drained, a long ridge stretching from Iceland to Antarctica would become visible at its bottom. South of the Azores are the so-called Atlantis seamounts. This is the dead body of legendary Atlantis.

Professor M. Ewing of Columbia University explored the mid-Atlantic Ridge in 1949. At the depth of between 2 and $3\frac{1}{2}$ miles he discovered pre-historic beach sand. This was a great riddle, as sand, being the product of erosion, is non-existent on the sea bed. The only conclusions that could have been reached about this discovery of sand at the bottom of the Atlantic are that either the land sank or that the ocean level was much lower in a past epoch. The last explanation brought up a question as to where all the extra water could have gone.

Many undersea valleys in the Atlantic are nothing else but continuations of existing rivers. This proves that in some places the sea bottom must have been land in the past. In

1898 a French cable ship found a piece of vitreous lava at the depth of 1,700 fathoms. This tachylyte is formed only above sea level. This means that a volcanic eruption occurred on the spot when the ocean bed was dry land.

The Andes must have risen abruptly in comparatively recent times when man could already navigate ships. If we reject this assumption, the presence of a sea harbour in Lake Titicaca at the altitude of 12,500 feet and 200 miles distant from the Pacific coast, is utterly inexplicable. The rings for cables on the piers were so large that they could have been used only by ocean-going vessels. Traces of seaweed and sea shells are still seen in this 'port' in the Andes. There are numerous raised beaches. The water in the southern portion of Lake Titicaca is still salty. Equally mysterious is the megalithic port of Nan-Matal in Ponape of the Carolines. Nan-Matal is a veritable Venice built out into the sea. Present-day natives do not claim that their forefathers built the harbour. They speak of the sun-kings who ruled over the island and sent ships to distant lands. Was Nan-Matal a large island, most of which sank when the Lake Titicaca port was raised? Quechua Indians say that corn was first grown near Lake Titicaca. Because of its high altitude, maize does not grow there today. All this suggests a sudden rise of the west coast of South America. The sinking of Atlantis could have caused the elevation of the Andes.

The Mexican explorer Jose Garcia Payon has found two huts in the Cordilleras under a thick layer of ice. Traces of shells spoke of a seashore on which these dwellings once stood. At the present time they rise almost 19,000 feet above sea level!

NEITH OF SAIS SPEAKS
It we turn to ancient literature, mythology and folklore, Atlantis becomes an historical possibility.

The *Timaeus* and *Critias* of Plato contain a chronicle of Atlantis. The story comes from Solon, the lawgiver of ancient Greece, who travelled to Egypt about 560 B.C.

The hieratic college of the goddess Neith of Sais, protectress of learning, confided to Solon that its archives were thousands of years old. These records spoke of a continent beyond the pillars of Hercules which sank about 9560 B.C.

Plato does not confuse Atlantis with America, as he distinctly says that there was a continent west of Atlantis. He speaks of an ocean beyond the Straits of Gibraltar and calls the Mediterranean "only a harbour". It is in that ocean—the Atlantic—that he places an island-continent larger than Libya and Asia Minor put together.

There was a fertile plain in the centre of Atlantis protected by lofty mountains from the northern winds. The climate was subtropical and Atlanteans gathered two crops a year. The country was rich in minerals, metals and agricultural produce. Industry, crafts and sciences flourished in Atlantis. It was proud of many fine harbours, docks and canals. Plato's mention of commercial links with the outside world indicates the use of ocean-going ships.

The people of Atlantis constructed their buildings of red, white and black stone. The temple of Cleito and Poseidon was surrounded by a golden fence, while the walls were made of silver and the building decorated with golden ornaments. It was there that the ten kings of Atlantis held their assemblies.

On the basis of Plato's data, the army and navy totalled 1,210,000 men. This figure suggests a multi-million population. During the last period of Atlantean history of which Plato speaks, the nation was ruled by the royal descendants of Poseidon. Shortly before its end, the Atlantean empire entered on a path of imperialism with the intention of expanding its colonies in the Mediterranean.

However, it appears from the account of Plato that in an earlier epoch the Atlanteans practised gentleness and wisdom. To quote him, "they despised everything but virtue", they thought "lightly on the possession of gold and other property, which seemed a burden to them; neither were they intoxicated by luxury; nor did wealth deprive them of their self-control". The people of Atlantis prized fellowship and friendship above worldly possessions. In the face of this contempt for private property and the sociality of Atlanteans, did they have a system of socialism in a bygone age? If so, the presence of a moneyless economy in the land of the Incas would be only natural, as Peru was, in all likelihood, a fragment of the Atlantean state.

According to Virgil's *Georgics* and Tibullus's *Elegies*, land in ancient times was held in common. Memories of a democracy in a former cycle were perpetuated in ancient Greece and Rome in the festivals of the Cronia and Saturnalia when masters and slaves drank and danced together for a day. The 5,000-year-old Engidu and the poem of Uttu of Sumer express lament for the lost social system in which "there were no liars, no sickness, nor old age".

Plato tells of the moral downfall of Atlanteans when avarice and egoism got the upper hand. Then Zeus "perceiving that an honourable race was in a most wretched state" and that they "aggressed wantonly against the whole of Europe and Asia", inflicted a terrible punishment on them. In the words of the Greek philosopher "the warlike men in a body sank into the earth and the island of Atlantis in like manner disappeared and was sunk beneath the sea".

Anticipating scepticism from his readers in future ages, Plato assures us that his story is "strange, yet perfectly true". Today his narrative is receiving more and more corroboration from science.

The sounding of the bed of the Atlantic reveals that there is a ridge stretching from north to south in the middle of the ocean. The Azores may be peaks of those submerged mountains which, in Plato's story, sheltered the central plain from cold northerly winds. From *Critias* we learn that Atlanteans built houses of white, black and red stone. Whitish calcareous terrains, black and red volcanic rocks are found on the Azores —the remnant of Atlantis.

In dealing with the problem of Atlantis it is not superfluous to mention the so-called Continental Drift theory of Professor Alfred Wegener, which postulates that 225 million years ago all the continents were united. The profile of the Americas and the geographical contours of Europe and Africa do indeed fit into each other.

This theory does not rule out the possible existence of Atlantis 12,000 years ago, for the simple reason that the Continental Drift takes millions of years. At the time of the sinking of Atlantis, Europe and America were only 2 kilometres closer.

There was plenty of room for Atlantis in the Atlantic Ocean at that time.

One more theory should not be bypassed. It is Professor Galanopoulos' opinion that Thira-Santorin was the site of Plato's Atlantis. This island in the Aegean Sea blew up in a geological disaster about 1400 B.C.

Plato indirectly received the original story of Atlantis from Solon, the great statesman and the richest man in ancient Greece. According to Solon, Atlantis perished 9,000 years before his trip to Egypt, or in 9560 B.C.

However, Professor Galanopoulos thinks that Solon, the Onassis of antiquity, could not even count properly. "It was not 9,000 years, but 900 years," he claims, adding 900 to 560 B.C., the date of Solon's voyage to Egypt, and getting 1460 B.C. or the time of Santorin's cataclysm. He believes Santorin was Atlantis. But this equation is very weak.

Plato writes in *Timaeus* that "in those days the Atlantic was navigable from an island situated to the west of the straits which you call the Pillars of Hercules (Gibraltar, A.T.). The island was larger than Libya and the Middle East." Plato calls the Atlantic a "true ocean". It is certainly not the Aegean Sea that he speaks of.

The Atlantis of Plato was approximately 600,000 square miles in area. The Santorin-Atlantis of Galanopoulos is only 75 square miles in size. Plato writes of the ten governors of Atlantis. But how could ten provinces have existed on Santorin?

The contradictions are too obvious. It is more than likely that Plato and Solon had better judgment than Galanopoulos.

ATLANTIS AND SCIENCE

Speculation as to a continent in the Atlantic which was the seat of a high civilization is well within the bounds of science. Academician V. A. Obrutchev of the U.S.S.R. was of the opinion that the legend of Atlantis was not "impossible or unacceptable from a geological standpoint".[2] Actually he was bold enough to say later that a probe of the northern portion of the

Atlantic Ocean "may reveal underwater ruins of buildings and other remains of an ancient culture".[3]

Professor N. Lednev, a Moscow physicist and mathematician, after twenty years of research has come to the conclusion that the fabled Atlantis is no myth. Lednev states that ancient historical documents and cultural monuments showed Atlantis was "a huge island extending for hundreds of kilometres, situated west of Gibraltar".[4] Another Soviet scientist, Ekaterina Hagemeister, wrote in 1955 that since the waters of the Gulf Stream reached the Arctic Ocean between 10,000 and 12,000 years ago, Atlantis must have been the barrier which had diverted the current to the south. "Atlantis was the cause of the appearance of the Ice Age. Atlantis was the cause of its end," she claimed.

Greenland has an ice-cap 5,000 feet deep and this never thaws. Norway is on the same latitude yet it has rich vegetation in summer. It is the Gulf Stream that warms up Scandinavia and the whole of Europe. This warm current is justly called the 'central heating' of Europe. The Swedish vessel *Albatross*, in sounding the bed of equatorial Atlantic, discovered traces of fresh-water plants at the depth of over 2 miles. Professor Hans Pettersson, who led the expedition, thought that an island had sunk on the spot.[5]

Foraminifera are tiny sea animals with a shell or test. There are two principal species—*Globorotalia menardii* and *Globorotalia truncatulinoides*. The first is distinguished by a shell coil spiralling leftwise and it lives in warm waters. The second is right-coiling and it can exist in cold ocean waters as well. These two species of sea animals can serve as indicators of climate, warm or cold. The warm type does not appear anywhere above the line stretching from the Azores to the Canaries. The cold-water foraminifera are present in the north-eastern quadrant of the Atlantic. The middle Atlantic zone, from West Africa to Central America, is inhabited by the warm type or *Globorotalia menardii*. Yet in the equatorial Atlantic the cold type shows up again. It looks as if the warm species of foraminifera tore through some barrier in an easterly direction. Was that barrier Atlantis?

The scientists working for Lamont Geological Observatory

in the United States have made an important discovery on the basis of foraminifera distribution: that a sudden warming of surface ocean waters took place in the Atlantic about 10,000 years ago. What is more, the transformation of the cold-type foraminifera into the warm one did not last more than a hundred years. The conclusion seems inescapable that some catastrophic changes in climate occurred in the Atlantic Ocean around 8000 B.C.

In the course of a submarine probe by the Geological Society of America in 1949, about a ton of limestone discs was lifted from the bed of the Atlantic, south of the Azores. Their average size was about 6 inches with a thickness of $1\frac{1}{2}$ inches. The discs had a peculiar cavity in the centre. On the outside they were relatively smooth, but in the cavities they were rough. These 'sea-biscuits' did not seem to be natural formations and could not be identified. According to Lamont Geological Observatory (Columbia University), "the state of lithification of the limestone suggests that it may have been lithified under subaerial conditions and that the seamount may have been an island within the past 12,000 years".[6]

In an attempt to ascertain the date of the sinking of Atlantis it should not be overlooked that the age of Niagara gorge (from the mouth of the river to the present waterfall) is 12,500 years, It is also a notable fact that the rise of the Cordilleras for 19,000 feet took place about 10,000 years ago.

Radio-carbon dating of different materials has given some highly significant results. An extensive cedar forest once grew on the Greater Bermuda, which is now under water. Carbon-14 test shows that the forest was wiped out about 11,000 years ago. Mud from Lake Knockacran in Ireland, traced to the last ice sheet, was found to be 11,787 years old. Spruce forest from Two Creeks, Wisconsin, was crushed by advancing glaciers about 11,000 years ago. Birch trees in North Germany were uprooted by moving ice masses about 10,800 years ago. Radio-carbon determination of the age of Jericho culture shows 6800 B.C. Artistic plaster skulls of refined people similar to the Egyptians have been found in Jericho. They lived 8,000 years ago.

From these figures it is obvious that a minor glaciation took place from 11,000 to 12,000 years ago. After this last advance of the glaciers from the polar cap, the climate became warmer. By 8000 B.C. in the so-called Mesolithic Age, the ice sheet retreated and opened the way to new lands for men, animals and plants. To recapitulate, the climates assumed their present characteristics between 10,000 and 8000 B.C. Europe and North America got considerably warmer than before. The Atlantis theory, which claims that the sunken continent blocked the path of the warm Gulf Stream to the North, can explain this climatic change.

But, unlike Europe, parts of Asia experienced changes of climate for the worse. In 1958 the Russian archaeologist V. A. Ranov found rock paintings in the Pamirs at the altitude of 14,000 feet—the highest in the world for any prehistoric art work. These drawings in the Shakhta cave, made with red mineral paint, depict a bear, boar and ostrich—none of which can at present survive in the arctic temperatures of the Pamirs.

A clue as to the age of the rock paintings was discovered in Markansu, where prehistoric settlers left artifacts and ash. The latter is from burnt birch and cedar which do not grow in the region today. Carbon-14 dating showed 9,500 years. This sudden freezing of the Pamirs may be due to a rapid elevation of the earth's crust in a geological upheaval.

A reindeer's skull has been found in the vicinity of Lake Sevan in rugged Soviet Armenia. The reindeer is an animal of the plains and its presence in the mountains of Southern Caucasus is a mystery. Has there been a geological cataclysm of such magnitude as to transform a plain into a mountainous country? Most scientists are not likely to entertain this idea, but the age of the skull has been estimated at 12,000 years— which tallies with the traditional date of the sinking of Atlantis.

When a carbon-14 test was made on a mammoth discovered in the northern part of Siberia, the result was 12,000 years. That thousands of mammoths died a sudden death is evident from the fact that some have been found with grasses in their mouths and stomachs, standing in an upright position.

It must be noted here that the mammoth was not a polar animal. In spite of longer hair, in structure and thickness its skin is similar to that of the tropical Indian elephant. The skin of these frozen animals is congested with red blood corpuscles. This is proof of death due to suffocation by water or gases.

For centuries ivory from the mammoths' tusks has constituted an item of trade. According to Richard Lydekker, approximately 20,000 pairs of tusks in perfect condition were sold in the few decades preceding 1899. This figure gives some idea as to the great number of frozen mammoths unearthed. It is important to emphasize here that ivory for carving can be used only from freshly killed animals, or those which have been frozen. Exposed tusks dry out and become valueless. Tens of thousands of mammoths have been discovered in northern areas of America and Asia. Since the mammoth ivory traded was of the best quality, there is no doubt that the beasts perished suddenly.

Professor Frank C. Hibben estimated that 40 million animals were exterminated in North America alone at the close of the Ice Age. "This death was catastrophic and all-inclusive," he writes.[7]

Carbon-14 tests reveal that the traces of man on the continent of America unexpectedly disappear about 10,400 years ago. Was it the legendary world flood that swept man off North America?

In this speculation, world population figures become very significant. About 2,000 years ago there were only 10 million people in the Americas. At the same time 26 million dwelt in Africa, 30 million in Europe and 133 million in Asia. These figures show that the Atlantic basin—America, Europe and Africa—had only half of the population of Asia. The remoteness from the arena of a geological disaster can account for the high figure of the population of Asia in ancient times.

THE ENIGMA OF THE BASQUES

The Basques have a legend of a cataclysm in which fire and water were at war. Their forebears hid themselves in caves and survived.

The Basque people speak a tongue which has an inexplicable affinity with American Indian dialects. A Basque missionary preached to the Indians in Peten, Guatemala in his native tongue and was understood.

The Basques believe in the mythical seven-headed serpent 'Erensuge' which links them with the snake-worshipping Aztecs on the other side of the Atlantic. The old Basque custom of counting by twenties instead of tens, has a parallel in Central America where a similar arithmetic was practised. Undoubtedly, the French have inherited their 'quatre-vingts' (four score or 80) from the Basques.

Likewise, the Basque ball game of 'jai alai', played with a wicker basket tied to the arm, is greatly reminiscent of the Maya game of 'pok-a-tok'.

When compared with other European peoples, the Basques stand unique in their common blood groups. They have a high frequency of group O, a relatively low frequency of group A, and the lowest frequency of group B in Europe. With regard to the Rh blood groups, they show the highest frequency in Rh-negatives found in any European population and, with the possible exception of some Berber tribes, the highest in the world. All this shows that the Basques are different from the French or Spanish.

The Basques of the Pyrenees are thought to be related to Cro-Magnons who occupied parts of France and Spain at the end of the Ice Age. They were unlike the aboriginal peoples of these countries, nor were they akin to any race in the east. Writing about the Basques in his *History of Spain* Rafael Altamira concludes that: "Perhaps they are the sole survivors of the prehistoric tribes that inhabited the caves of the Pyrenees and left so many evidences of artistic ability and technical skill." [8]

The Basques, alone of the peoples of Western Europe, have preserved animal and totem dances of primitive races. They cherished a belief in the immortality of the unburied body, shared by ancient Egyptians and Incas. The custom of artificial flattening of the head was upheld by the Basques as well as by the Indians of Central America.

The Cro-Magnons were six-footers with a larger brain case than the man of today—a surprising trait to discover in a cave-dweller. With full and smooth forehead and prominent cheekbones, they resembled the Guanches of the Canary Islands, who are suspected of being Atlantean descendants. The Cro-Magnons were talented artists yet their tools and weapons were made of stone. For lack of suitable materials to which they had been accustomed in their homeland, the race used stone, shaped into articles on the patterns from their mother culture.

Rock paintings, engravings and sculptures of Cro-Magnons in the Magdalenian epoch, about 11,000 or more years ago, stand superb in the history of art. If their culture was not a legacy, it is difficult to see how these cavemen in the Biscay could have developed artistic talent which was superior to that of ancient Egypt or Sumer in its dynamic realism and dramatic representation.

Azilians, a prehistoric race in Spain, were invariably buried with their faces towards the west. They were noted for their skill in fishing and seafaring. Did they come from a western land in ships?

DOOMSDAY

It is Ovid, the Roman poet, who writes about the Great Flood and continues the unfinished chronicle of Plato:

> There was such wickedness once on earth that Justice fled to the sky, and the king of the gods determined to make an end of the race of men. . . . Jupiter's anger was not confined to his province of the sky. Neptune, his sea-blue brother, sent the waves to help him. Neptune smote the earth with his trident and the earth shivered and shook. . . . Soon there was no telling land from sea. Under the water the sea nymphs Nereides were staring in amazement at woods, houses and cities. Nearly all men perished by water, and those who escaped the water, having no food, died of hunger.

From ancient Egyptian sources we learn that Nu, the god of waters, advised his son Ra, the sun-god, to wholly destroy mankind when the nations revolted against the gods. It can be concluded from this record that this destruction was accomplished by an inundation by Nu, the ruler of the seas.

A 3,000-year-old twelfth Dynasty papyrus preserved at the Leningrad Hermitage mentions the "Island of the Serpent" and contains this passage: "After you leave my island you will not find it again as this place will vanish under the sea waves."

The ancient Egyptian document describes the fall of a meteor and the catastrophe which followed: "Once a star fell from heaven and the flames consumed everything. All were burned but I alone was saved. However, when I saw the mountain of corpses I almost died of grief."

It is well nigh impossible to visualize the geological upheavals which destroyed Atlantis. Folklore and sacred scriptures of many races draw dramatic pictures of the cataclysm.

The 4,000-year-old *Epic of Gilgamesh* contains a detailed account of the Flood and thus laments the end of an archaic people: "Would that famine had wasted the world, rather than the Flood."

The Bible has the story of Noah's Ark and the Great Flood. In the Book of Enoch, the patriarch who had warned Noah of the approaching disaster before being taken to heaven alive, there are meaningful passages about "the fire of the west" and "the great sea towards the west".

About eighteen hundred years ago Lucian recorded a remarkable story which illustrates how strong the traditions of the Great Flood were in antiquity. The priests of Baalbek, now in the Lebanon, had the curious custom of pouring sea water from the Mediterranean into a cleft in the rock near the temple to perpetuate the memory of the waters of the Deluge pouring away into it, as also the rescue of Deucalion. To get this sea water, the priests had to travel to the seashore of the Mediterranean and then back to Baalbek, for as long as four days. It is worthy to remark that this cleft is the northern end of the Great Rift which extends as far south as the Zambezi River. This priest rite may be a folk memory of a great cataclysm.

A Bushmen's tale points to a vast island which had existed west of Africa but was later submerged. This is one of the many legends about the sinking of Atlantis.

Extraordinary testimonies of a world cataclysm exist on the

other side of the Atlantic. This is but natural if it is assumed that Atlantis was linked by commercial and cultural ties with Europe and Africa as well as with the Americas.

A Maya codex states that "the sky approached the earth and in one day all perished. Even the mountains disappeared under water." The Dresden Codex of the Mayas shows the destruction of the world in pictorial form. On the chart there is a serpent in the sky with torrents of water pouring out from its mouth. Mayan signs indicate lunar and solar eclipses. The moon goddess, the patroness of death, has a frightening appearance. An inverted bowl, from which gushes a destroying flood, is in her hands.[9]

The *Popol Vuh*, the sacred book of Guatemala Mayas, bears witness to the dire character of the disaster. It says that the roar of fires was heard above. The earth shook and things revolted against man. It rained tar with water. The trees were swinging, houses crumbling, caves collapsing. Then day became black night. The *Chilam Balam* of Yucatan asserts that the motherland of the Mayas was swallowed up by the sea amid earthquakes and fiery eruptions in a very distant epoch. A white Indian tribe, Paria, used to live in Venezuela, in a village with so significant a name as Atlan. They had a tradition of a calamity which had destroyed their country, a large island in the ocean. A perusal of American Indian mythology discloses an interesting fact that over 130 tribes have legends of a world catastrophe.

Can mythology and folklore be used to some extent in filling the numerous gaps in history? Professor I. A. Efremov of the Soviet Union answers in the affirmative. He insists that "historians must pay more respect to ancient traditions and folklore". Efremov accuses scientists in the West of a certain snobbishness when it comes to the tales of the so-called common people.

An Eskimo legend says: "Then a mighty flood came. Many men were drowned and they grew fewer." Eskimos and Chinese have a curious myth that the earth had tilted violently before the Flood.

An earth-axis tilt can explain a world-wide cataclysm, but science knows of no causes which could produce such sudden wobbling. A collision with a huge meteor may have triggered the Atlantean cataclysm or, according to the Hoerbiger Theory, the capture of a planet, now known as the moon. Carolina 'bays' are thought by some scientists to be meteoric scars. On the average, these elliptical craters are about half a mile in diameter, with elevated rims and depressions 25 to 50 feet deep. Incidentally, a very large number of meteorites have been found in North and South Carolina.

The hypothesis of the shifting crust, offered by Dr Charles H. Hapgood of U.S.A., deserves a serious consideration. He theorizes that the thin terrestrial crust slides back and forth on the molten ball. It is the weight of the ice-caps on the poles that sets the sliding in motion. Dr Hapgood can account for the presence of coral fossils in the Arctic or the northward movements of glaciers in the Himalayas.

If the earth's shell is movable, a collision with an asteroid could have been instrumental in displacing the crust. This is not science fiction but an astronomical possibility—let us recall how our planet missed such a collision with a planetoid in October 1937 by only five and a half hours.

Professor N. S. Vetchinkin of Russia has an answer to the riddle of Atlantis and the world deluge: "The fall of a gigantic meteorite was the cause of the destruction of Atlantis. Impacts of gigantic meteorites are clearly seen on the surface of the moon. There are craters 200 kilometres in diameter, whereas on earth they are only 3 kilometres wide. Falling into the sea, gigantic meteorites brought about tidal waves which washed away not only the plant and animal kingdoms but also hills and mountains." [10]

The memory of Atlantean cataclysm is still alive in the myths of many peoples. It can be deduced from their study that the scope and character of the catastrophe varied with geographical locations.

The Quiche Indians of Guatemala remember a black rain which fell from the sky at the time of an earthquake destroying houses and caves. This implies that violent tectonic movements occurred in the Atlantic. Smoke, ashes and steam from the boiling sea went into the stratosphere, then drifted westward because of the rotation of the earth, bringing about this black rain over Central America. The Quiche legends are confirmed by those of the Amazon Indians. After a terrific explosion the world was plunged into darkness, they say. The Peruvian Indians add that water rose to the height of the mountains.

In the Mediterranean basin we hear more about floods than volcanic phenomena. In ancient Greek mythology tidal waves cover the tops of trees leaving fishes gasping in the branches when water subsides. The Zend Avesta affirms that in Persia the Flood reached up to a man's height.

Travelling farther east, we find that in China the sea receded towards the south-east, as the ancient documents state. This sketch of the world cataclysm is quite consistent. A gigantic tide in the Atlantic was likely to produce an ebb on the other face of the globe—the Pacific Ocean.

Interesting supporting arguments are worth mentioning. In ancient Mexico there was a holiday devoted to a past event in which constellations had assumed a new aspect. It follows that in a bygone age the heavens did not have the same appearance as now.

Martinus Martini, seventeenth-century Jesuit missionary in China, wrote in *History of China* concerning her oldest records. These speak of a time when the sky suddenly began to fall northward. The sun, moon and planets changed their courses, after the earth had been shaken. This is certainly a strong hint at the wobble of the earth for it alone can explain the astronomical phenomena described in Chinese writings.

Two star maps painted on the ceiling of the tomb of Senmouth, Queen Hatshepsut's architect, present a riddle. The cardinal points are correctly placed on one of these astronomical charts but on the other they are reversed, as if the earth had undergone a tilt. In fact, the Harris Papyrus mentions that the earth had turned over in a cosmic cataclysm. The Hermitage Papyrus of Leningrad and the Ipuwer Papyrus also allude to the world having been turned upside down.

The Indians living in the lower reaches of Mackenzie River in northern Canada maintain that during the Deluge an unbearable heat wave came upon their arctic land. Suddenly the heat was followed by a severe frost. A displacement of the atmosphere in an earth tilt could have brought about the weather extremes spoken of by the Canadian Indians.

It appears from the testimony of the ages that the Doomsday of Atlantis was violent and terrible.

PYRAMIDS AND CONQUISTADORES

A mighty empire in the middle of the Atlantic Ocean must have had colonies in Europe, Africa and America. There are facts to substantiate this viewpoint.

Ancient Egypt constructed colossal pyramids. Babylon had ziggurats or tiered towers where astronomical studies were combined with religious worship. The ancient inhabitants of Central and South America also built huge pyramids used as temples, observatories or tombs. It is a long way from Babylon and Egypt to Mexico, yet this custom of pyramid-building on both sides of the Atlantic can be comprehended on the assumption that it had originated in Atlantis, from which it spread eastward and westward.

It is generally thought that pyramids are merely expressions of an urge to erect artificial mountains. This may be true of flat Egypt or Mesopotamia but the theory does not explain the presence of similar pyramids in the rugged lands of Mexico and Peru. Evidently there are other reasons for the construction of identical pyramids on both sides of the Atlantic. A tradition from Atlantis may be one reason.

According to Josephus Flavius, a Jewish historian of the first century, Nimrod built the Tower of Babel for the purpose of providing shelter should another deluge sweep the earth. The Mexican chronicler Ixtlilxochitl passes on to us a parallel Toltec motive for the construction of pyramids: "After men had multiplied, they erected a very high 'zacuali', which is today a tower of great height, in order to take refuge in it should the second world be destroyed."

Critical scientists insist that the pyramids appeared in Asia, Africa and America independently—not from a common source, as Atlantologists believe.

However, without a common source why should the purpose of the pyramids be identical in Babylon and Mexico? Josephus and Ixtlilxochitl define it very clearly—to provide shelter should another deluge sweep the world.

The Central Americans had always expected the end of the world—hence the origin of human sacrifices of the Aztecs made to placate the angry gods and save mankind from another calamity.

Olmechs, the predecessors of Mayas and Aztecs, may have been subjects of the Atlantean Empire. When archaeologists failed to find out the age of the Pyramid of Ciucuilco in the vicinity of Mexico City, they called on the geologists for assistance, as half of the structure was covered with solid lava. Since there are two volcanoes nearby, the natural question was: "When did the eruption take place?" The answer was staggering: "Eight thousand years ago." [11] If this conclusion is correct, a high civilization had existed in Central America in remotest antiquity.

Like the pyramids, sphinxes are found in Yucatan, where they are rendered in Mayan style.

Many Atlantologists consider that the emblem of the cross had come from Atlantis because all of its presumed colonies worshipped the sign. In ancient America the cross was a favourite symbol. On Egyptian murals many gods are depicted with the Tau cross as well as the Maltese cross. Assyrian and Babylonian monarchs and warriors used to wear crosses on their necks as sacred talismans.

The sun cult was received by ancient peoples from Atlantis. The adoration of the sun in Egypt and Peru, and the reign of solar dynasties, are quoted by Atlantologists as examples. The Turin Papyrus speaks of Ra, the sun-god. It also mentions a great calamity with floods and fires. From this some researchers conclude that the cult of the sun had been imported into Egypt from doomed Atlantis.

Egyptians believed in Amenti, the land of the dead in the west. If the Kingdom of the Dead means the sunken kingdom of Atlantis, then the fabulous dynasty of demigods in Egypt is the dynasty of the sovereigns of Atlantis. Ancient tradition tells us that five hundred years before the final catastrophe, the Atlantean kings moved to Egypt and founded the Dynasty of the Dead, foreseeing the doom of their continent.

Aztec priests zealously preserved the memory of Aztlan, a country in the east where Quetzalcoatl had come from as a culture bearer. Incas believed in Viracocha, who had arrived from the land of dawn. Earlier Egyptian records speak of Thoth or Tehuti, who came from a western land to plant civilization and learning on the soil of the Valley of the Nile.

Ancient Greeks sang of the Elysian Fields on the Isle of the Blest in the remote west. According to them, Tartarus, the home of the dead, was situated under the mountains of an island in the western ocean. Ancient Greeks and Egyptians pointed to the west in placing this mysterious island. American Indians gestured towards the east to indicate the location of the country of Quetzalcoatl or Viracocha. The land west of the Mediterranean and east of the Americas was nothing but Atlantis, the dead continent submerged in the ocean.

Though many nations of antiquity had religions with a belief in the immortality of the soul, only Peruvians and Egyptians maintained that the soul hovered near the dead body and was connected with it. Both races recognized the necessity to preserve the corpse by means of embalming.

The tradition of divine kings in the east was largely responsible for the defeat of Aztecs and Incas by a handful of conquistadores. When Columbus reached the West Indies and landed with his men "the natives carried them around on their arms, kissed their hands and feet, and in short, tried to make clear to them in every possible way that it was known the white man came from the gods".[12]

Montezuma, the last king of the Aztecs, told Cortes that "our fathers were not born here but they came from a distant country called Aztlan, with a high mountain and a garden where the gods lived". Montezuma also said that he reigned only as a viceroy of Quetzalcoatl, the ruler of an eastern empire. The Maya book *Popol Vuh* attests to the ancient custom of princes to travel east across the sea in order to "receive the investiture of the kingdom".

The easy victories of Cortes and Pizarro are the best proof of the actual existence of Atlantis in the dim past. The Aztec and Inca tradition cherished by the priests, worshipped great masters in the land of sunrise who were tall, white-skinned and bearded. When the adventurous Spaniards arrived on the scene, they were immediately identified as representatives of the legendary empire in the Atlantic. At first, the peoples of Montezuma and Atahualpa received the white men with open arms because they had been expected for so long.

This strong faith in a master state in the land of dawn is one of the principal causes of the collapse of the powerful empires of Mexico and Peru. The expectation of regular visitations of American colonies by Atlantean emperors proved fatal to the civilizations of the New World.

Cristobal Molina, a Spanish priest at Cuzco, Peru, wrote in the sixteenth century that it was from Manco Copac that the Incas had the full story of the Great Deluge.

Traditionally, there existed a planetary state with one language before the Flood. That state was certainly the fabulous Atlantis. Though separated by a vast distance, Israel and Babylon in Asia Minor and Mexico in Central America have preserved this belief in their sacred writings.

The Bible describes a time when there was only one race and language in the world. After the erection of the tower of Babel, people ceased to understand each other as many dialects appeared. The Babylonian historian Berosus records an epoch in which a past nation was so proud of its power and glory that it began to despise the gods. In Babylon a tall tower, almost touching the sky, was built. But the winds came to the assistance of the gods and overturned the tower. Its ruins came to be known as 'Babel'. Until then mankind spoke but one tongue. Strange as it sounds, the Toltec chronicles of Mexico contain a practically identical account of the construction of a high pyramid and the appearance of many languages.

If the story of the tower of Babel is not a fable but history, then indeed there was a global empire with one world language in a forgotten epoch.

As a planetary state could not have existed without organized lines of communication and an advanced technology, an astounding possibility of the presence of science in a pre-

33

historic, antediluvian age looms on the horizon. It is highly significant that more kinds of food and medical plants were cultivated by agriculturists of Central and South America than by any other race on our planet. In the pre-Inca and Inca epochs 240 varieties of potatoes and 20 types of maize were developed in the Andes and Upper Amazon. The cucumbers and tomatoes in our salads, potatoes, pumpkin and beans in our entrées, strawberries and chocolate in our desserts, came originally from the New World. In fact, half of the things we eat today were unknown till the discovery of America. Did ancient Peru and Mexico inherit the science of agriculture from Atlantis?

CALENDARS FROM ATLANTIS

Across the Atlantic there is another link between ancient Egypt and Peru. Their calendars had eighteen months of twenty days with a five-day holiday at the end of the year. Is this coincidence or tradition from a common source?

The approximate date of the end of Atlantis can be arrived at from the examination of ancient calendars. The first year of Zoroastrian chronology is 9660 B.C. when "time began". This is very close to the date given by Egyptian priests to Solon for the doomsday of Atlantis, or 9560 B.C.

Ancient Egyptians calculated time in 1,460-year solar cycles. The end of their last astronomical epoch came in A.D. 139. Eight solar cycles from this date can be traced back to the year 11,542 B.C. The lunar calendar of Assyrians divided time in periods of 1,805 years. The last one ended in 712 B.C. Six lunar cycles from this date are followed back to 11,542 B.C. The solar calendar of Egypt and the lunar calendar system of Assyria coincided in the same year—11,542 B.C., when both calendars were presumably created.

The Brahmins measure time in rounds of 2,850 years from 3102 B.C. Three of these cycles, or 8,550 years, added to 3102 B.C. give us the date of 11,652 B.C.

The Mayan calendar shows that the ancient peoples of Central America had long cycles of 2,760 years. The beginning of one span is traced to the year 3373 B.C. Three periods of 2,760 years, or 8,280 years from 3373 B.C. would take us back

34

to 11,653 B.C. which, within a year is the same date as that of the sages of India.

Vatican Codex A-3738 contains a significant chronology of the Aztecs according to which the first cycle continued for 4,008 years ending in a flood. The second of 4,010 years was destroyed by hurricanes. The third era of 4,801 years was closed by fires. In the fourth period which lasted 5,042 years, mankind suffered starvation. The present era is the fifth and it began in 751 B.C. The duration of all the four periods listed in this Codex is 17,861 years; and its beginning is traced to an incredibly distant date of 18,612 B.C.

Bishop Diego de Landa wrote in 1566 that in his time the Mayas reckoned their calendar from a date which was about 3113 B.C. in European chronology. They claimed that 5,125 years had passed before this date in former cycles. This would move the origin of the early Mayas to 8238 B.C., or close to the period of Atlantean cataclysm.

Aside from providing a clue as to the dating of Atlantis, a reasonable supposition can be made on the basis of these figures that many thousand years ago mankind possessed a considerable knowledge of astronomy which is usually characteristic of a high civilization.

The longest day in the Mayan calendar contained 13 hours and the shortest 11. In Ancient Egypt the longest day had 12 hours 55 minutes and the shortest 11 hours 5 minutes. These figures are almost identical with the Mayan hours. But what is really puzzling is this—12 hours 55 minutes is not actually the duration of the longest day in Egypt but in the Sudan. In an attempt to explain this difference, Dr L. Zajdler of Warsaw suggests that this time reckoning had come from tropical Atlantis.[13]

Archaeologist Arthur Posnansky of La Paz, Bolivia, speaking of the uncompleted Sun Temple at Tiahuanaco, claims that the construction was suddenly abandoned about 9550 B.C. The date is familiar—the priests of Sais told Solon that Atlantis perished in 9560 B.C.

In the words of E. F. Hagemeister of U.S.S.R. science has this to say about the sinking of Atlantis: "The end of the European Ice Age, appearance of the Gulf Stream and submergence of Atlantis occurred simultaneously about 10,000 B.C."

Not all scientists take a similar stand in the problem of Atlantis. Some discard the theory altogether in spite of all the evidence. Others attempt to put Atlantis in the Mediterranean, Spain or Germany. Needless to say, this is not the Atlantis of Plato and Egyptian scholars which they placed "in front of the Pillars of Hercules in the Atlantic sea".

In the Egyptian section of the Louvre in Paris I saw a carved design inconspicuously exhibited in a staircase with no tablet. However, I recognized the carving as the famous Denderah Zodiac. Originally this ancient Egyptian relic was part of a ceiling in the portico of the temple of Denderah in Upper Egypt. It was brought to France by Lelorrain in 1821.

For many generations the Calendar of Denderah has remained a baffling riddle to science. The zodiacal signs are arranged in a spiral and the symbols are easily recognizable, but Leo is at the point of vernal equinox. Because of the precession of equinoxes this would indicate a date between 10,950 to 8800 B.C., or the period during which the Atlantean catastrophe took place.

The Zodiac of Denderah is of Egyptian origin but it may have been engraved to commemorate a distant event—the end of Atlantis and the birth of a new cycle.

CHAPTER TWO

EXODUS

BY ARK AND AIRCRAFT

Mythology and ancient writings show that the last day of Atlantis was a veritable doomsday. Mountain-like ocean waves, hurricanes and volcanic explosions swept over the planet. Civilization came to a standstill and remaining mankind was reduced to a barbaric state.

The Sumerian tablets of Gilgamesh speak of Utnapishtim, primeval ancestor of humanity, who with his family was the only survivor of a vast flood. He saved his people, animals and birds in an ark. The biblical account of Noah appears to be a later version of the same story.

In the Zend Avesta of Iran we find another rendering of the Flood legend. Yima, a Persian patriarch, was ordered by the god Ahuramazda to prepare for a world deluge. Accordingly, Yima constructed a cavern where animals and plants useful to man were enclosed during the inundation. This is how civilization was revived after the destruction wrought by the Flood.

The Mahabharata of India relates how Brahma, taking the shape of a fish, warned Manu, the father of the human race, of the approaching flood. Manu was instructed to build a ship and take in "the seven Rishis (sages) and all the different seeds enumerated by Brahmins of yore and preserve them carefully". Manu followed the orders of Brahma and the vessel carrying him, the seven wise men and the seeds intended for the rehabilitation of survivors, travelled for years on the heaped-up waters until it landed in the Himalayas. Traditional lore of India points to Manali in the Kulu Valley, the town of Manu, as the possible spot where Manu disembarked. The district is generally known as Aryavarta, the land of the Aryans. It is in Manali in the Himalayas that this chapter is written.

The resemblance of the rescue of Noah to that of Manu, does not seem to be coincidental. It is a notable fact that in all these records of the Great Flood, certain chosen persons are attributed with a foreknowledge of the approaching world calamity.

The escape from the doomed land of Atlantis was effected in aircraft as well as sea vessels. There are numerous historical traditions to back this seemingly fantastic theory. Eskimos have a curious legend that they had been transported to the frozen north by giant metallic birds. Does this not suggest the presence of airships in the prehistory of man?

Aborigines of Northern Territory in Australia have a tale of the Flood and the Bird-Men. Karan, a chief, gave wings to Waark and Weirk when "the water filled up the creek and the sea came up and covered all the country, the hills, the trees, everything". Then Karan himself flew away and sat down alongside the moon, as the Bird-People watched him.[14]

The *Epic of Gilgamesh* paints a dramatic picture of the day of planetary disaster:

> From the foundations of heaven a black cloud arose.
> All that is bright is turned into darkness.
> The brother seeth his brother no more.
> The folk of the skies can no longer recognize each other.
> The gods feared the flood.
> They fled, they climbed into the heaven of Anu.

Who were the 'folk of the skies'? Who were the gods fearing the Flood and finding refuge in the heavens? If they were ethereal beings, they would not have been terrified by the fury of the elements. It appears that the sky-people were none other than Atlantean leaders who possessed aircraft or even spaceships. In Sumerian religion the 'heaven of Anu' was the abode of Anu, the father of gods. Its meaning was associated with the words 'great above' and 'depths'. Nowadays we call this—space. The sky-people departed into space—such is our interpretation of the puzzling passage of the epic.

The *Book of Dyzan*, received by Helena Blavatsky from a

Himalayan hermitage about a hundred years ago, may be a lost page from the history of mankind: "The first Great Waters came. They swallowed the Seven Great Islands. All holy saved, the unholy destroyed." [15]

The ancient commentary to the book is quite clear about the manner in which the exodus was carried out in Atlantis. The Great King of the Dazzling Face, the leader of the enlightened in Atlantis, seeing the inevitability of a catastrophe sent his airships to his brother-chiefs with the following message: "Prepare, arise ye men of the Good Law, and cross the land while dry." This plan must have been materialized in secret from the powerful evil rulers of the empire. Then one dark night, as the people of the 'Good Law' were far away beyond the danger of tidal waves, their great king assembled his vassals, fell upon his 'dazzling face' and wept. As the hour had struck, the princes embarked 'vimanas' (airships) and followed their tribes to the lands of the east and north, or Africa and Europe. In the meantime, meteorites showered on the kingdom of Atlantis where the 'unholy' ones slept.

That the possibility of exodus from Atlantis in airships is worthy of scientific speculation, if not necessarily acceptance, can be seen from the inclusion of an illustration in the *Interplanetary Travel Encyclopaedia* compiled by Professor N. A. Rynin of U.S.S.R., which depicts the pick-up of Atlantean high priests by an aircraft on the background of sinking Atlantis.

It is certain that only few people possessed aircraft or spaceships in the pre-deluge era. In our own day aeroplanes and space rockets are owned by big companies and the state. The situation may have been very much the same in Atlantean times.

Babylonians had preserved the memory of prehistoric astronauts or aviators in the image of Etana, the flier. The Berlin Museum has a seal cylinder which shows him soaring in the sky on an eagle's back, between the sun and the moon.

In Palenque, Mexico there is an intriguing design on a sarcophagus in a pyramid discovered by archaeologist Ruz-Lhuillier. In Maya style it shows a man sitting in a rocket-like machine with a fiery exhaust. He is leaning forward and his hands rest on handles. The rocket cone contains many enigmatic objects which could be parts of its mechanism. After analyzing numerous codices Tarade and Millou of France made a conclusion that this is a Maya concept of an astronaut in a spaceship.[16]

The hieroglyphics on the border stand for the sun, moon and the star Polaris—which lend support to the 'cosmic' interpretation. On the other hand, the two dates on the tomb—A.D 603 and 633 make it dubious. However, if the priest buried in the grave was not only an astronomer-priest but custodian of the Central American tradition about 'astral gods', then this ornament may be a memento of their space travels.

A tradition of aerial vehicles in antiquity may be a dim echo from prehistoric aviation and astronautics. Since some Atlantologists maintain that there had been a high civilization before the Flood, this explanation may not be too far off the mark.

ATOMIC BOMBS AND SPACESHIPS BEFORE THE FLOOD

What was the shape of things in Atlantis shortly before the cataclysm? Plato definitely speaks of conquests and imperialism of Atlanteans in their closing epoch.

The Samsaptakabadha scripture of India mentions airships powered by "celestial forces". It speaks of a missile which contained the "power of the universe". The blaze of the explosion is compared to "ten thousand suns". The book says: "The gods had become alarmed and cried: Do not burn the whole world to ashes."

The Sanskrit *Mausola Purva* refers to "an unknown weapon, an iron thunderbolt, a gigantic messenger of death which reduced to ashes the entire races of the Vrishnis and the Anhakas. The corpses were so burned as to be unrecognizable. Their hair and nails fell out; pottery broke without any apparent cause and the birds turned white. After a few hours, all foodstuffs were infected."

Alexander Gorbovsky writes in his *Riddles of Antiquity* that a human skeleton found in India was radioactive. Its radioactivity was fifty times above the normal. One begins to wonder if the *Mausola Purva* is history rather than legend.

40

Speaking of charred Borsippa, which is often identified with the ruins of the Tower of Babel, E. Zehren in *Die Biblischen Hügel* asks what power could have melted the bricks of the ziggurat. The answer is—nothing but a monster thunderbolt or an atom bomb.

Professor Frederick Soddy, Nobel Prize winner and the discoverer of isotopes, speaking of the traditions which have been handed down to us from a prehistoric time, wrote in 1909: "Can we not read into them some justification for the belief that some former forgotten race of men attained not only to the knowledge we have so recently won, but also to the power that is not yet ours".[17]

In 1909 that power, the power of the atom was not ours. It is obvious that Professor Soddy envisaged a past civilization which had mastered atomic energy. In discussing this prehistoric race, the pioneer nuclear scientist also imagined that "possibly they could explore the outer realms of space".

Ancient books of India speak of aeroplanes, atomic bombs as well as space travel. A Vedic god Pushan sails in golden ships across the ocean of the sky. Garuda, a celestial bird, carries Lord Vishnu in cosmic travels. The *Samsaptakabadha* describes aerial flights "through the region of the sky firmament which is above the region of the winds". This is a clear indication of space travel. The *Surya Siddhanta*, the oldest Sanskrit work on astronomy, cites Siddhas or perfect men and Vidhyaharas or possessors of knowledge who travel around the earth "below the moon and above the clouds". Is this not a definite suggestion of philosophers and scientists orbiting around our planet?

If the *Epic of Gilgamesh* is linked with the Indian scriptures many gaps in the history of early man became filled. At the time of world cataclysm the 'sky-folk' of the Gilgamesh departed heavenward either to orbit around the earth or even to fly to other planets. The *Samaranagana Sutrahara* says that by means of skyships men could fly in the air and also 'heavenly beings' could reach the earth. One can not help thinking of a two-way traffic between our planet and other worlds, reading this passage.

It is more reasonable to suppose that the exodus from Atlantis was carried out by boats, rather than by airships or spacecraft which were reserved for the privileged. The refugees settled in the neighbouring Pyrenees and Egypt providing an impetus to the civilizations of the Mediterranean basin.

CHAPTER THREE

ANTEDILUVIAN COLONIES

A STATE ABOUT WHICH U.N.O. KNOWS NOTHING

A German author K. K. Doberer, writing in *The Goldmakers*, expresses this thought: "One possibility, in the view of the wise men of Atlantis, was to escape from the peril by migration—by pushing through the Mediterranean, on and on to the east, into the land-masses of Asia and founding colonies on the 'Roof of the World'."

This is a startling conjecture and perhaps not very far from truth. The highpriests and princes of the 'Good Law' could have been airlifted to a remote and safe part of the globe with all the fruits of their culture and technology. In small, completely isolated communities they might have developed their science to heights undreamt of even by our academies. There is evidence to give weight to this apparently fantastic theory.

In the *Epic of Mahabharata* we read of an archaic era in which airships flew in the sky and devastating bombs were dropped on cities. Brutal wars were fought and evil reigned unchecked. From ancient writings and legends of many races it is possible to restore the picture of what had probably taken place shortly before the geological catastrophe.

When a band of illumined philosophers and scientists had realized that culture was doomed and the progress of mankind imperilled, they decided to withdraw into inaccessible parts of the world. Secret underground shelters were built in the mountains. Hidden valleys in the Himalayas had been allocated for the chosen few who were to carry the torch of enlightenment into the future.

When the ocean engulfed Atlantis, the surviving colonies were left intact to build a utopia, avoiding the mistakes of the destroyed empire. Away from barbarism and ignorance, these communities prospered in protective isolation. It was resolved

43

from the start to sever all connection with the outside world. Unencumbered their science flourished, surpassing the achievements of Atlantis.

Fantasy? Yet a number of present-day scientists have already suggested underground shelters and even subterranean cities in anticipation of an atomic holocaust. Depopulation of cities and construction of underground towns—are the projects offered by responsible men of science in an attempt to ensure the continuation of the human race. If this plan is contemplated by today's scientists, is it not possible that a similar project was proposed and carried out by the cultural leaders of Atlantis when confronted with the moral degeneration of mankind and the menace of 'Brahma's weapon', which blazed like ten thousand suns?

The picture of a powerful state with an advanced technology in a forgotten epoch is well within the framework of sane scientific thinking. Professor Frederick Soddy, a pioneer nuclear physicist, in an endeavour to explain scientific tradition of the ancients, said in 1909 that "it may be an echo from one of many previous epochs in the unrecorded history of the world, of an age of men which have trod before the road we are treading today".[17]

To preserve the products of civilization for an indefinite period against the dangers of devastating wars and geological calamities, nothing would be more effective than underground shelters. This is as true today as it was in the days of Atlantis.

From the story of man's life on this planet many pages have been torn out by the hand of Time. However, legend speaks of a colossal disaster which wiped out an advanced civilization. Most of the survivors became savages. Those who were later rehabilitated by 'divine messengers' rose from their primitive state and gave birth to the nations of ancient history from which we ourselves derive our origins. The secret communities of the 'Children of the Sun' were small in number but great in knowledge. By means of their high science they excavated a vast network of tunnels, particularly in Asia.

Isolation has been the eternal law of these colonies. Philosophers, scientists, poets, artists, religious devotees, writers and musicians require a peaceful environment in which to pursue their labours. They do not want to hear the tramping of soldiers' boots or the cries of the market place. No one can accuse these philosophers of the vice of selfishness because down through the ages they had shared their wisdom with those who were ready for it. This detachment is of a protective nature. For is not the rule of the fist as strong today as in the times of Caligula? Perhaps, the fist is even more awful in its technological armour.

Lost in the secret valleys between snowy ridges or hidden in mountain catacombs live the Elder Brothers of the human race. Indications of the reality of these colonies came from such widely separated countries as India, America, Tibet, Russia, Mongolia and other parts of the world. Over the expanse of time these reports have appeared in the past five thousand years. Embellished by fancy of the people living in various lands, they contain grains of truth.

Dr. Ferdinand Ossendowski of the Académie Française wrote of a strange story related to him by Prince Chultun Beyli and his chief Lama in Mongolia, some fifty years ago. Two continents had formerly existed in the Atlantic and the Pacific. They sank into the sea depths, but some of their inhabitants found refuge in vast underground shelters. These caves are flooded with a peculiar light which affords growth to the plants and gives life to this lost tribe of pre-historic mankind. The race has reached the highest levels of science.[18]

The Polish savant states that the subterranean people of Agharti have great technical achievements. They possess unusual cars which travel with great speed through a huge network of tunnels in Asia. They have made a study of life on other planets. But their greatest accomplishments are in the realm of the mind.

In his travels through Chinese Turkestan or Sinkiang, the famous explorer and artist Nicholas Roerich was shown long underground corridors. Local inhabitants told him that strange people had emerged from the catacombs to shop in towns. They had paid for goods with ancient coins which no one could identify. While stopping at Tsagan Kure near Kalgan in China in 1935 Roerich wrote an article—"The Guardians". He questions if mysterious men appear in the middle of the desert

45

as if out of nowhere, could they not have come out of some subterranean passage? [19] Nicholas Roerich asked the Mongols about these mystery visitors. They made known to him many interesting facts. The strangers occasionally would come on horseback. In order not to stir too much curiosity they were dressed like merchants, cattlemen or soldiers. Gifts had been received by Mongols from them.[19]

The testimony of a man of international repute and scholarly and artistic accomplishments can not be dismissed lightly. The author had the great privilege of meeting the explorer in Shanghai, China after his expedition of 1935.

It should be mentioned here that Professor Roerich and the members of his team watched a shiny disc over Karakoram Range in 1926. It was a sunny morning and the object was clearly seen with the three pairs of powerful binoculars available. The circular craft then abruptly changed its course. Forty years ago there were no planes or balloons in Central Asia. Was this an airship from a prehistoric colony?

When the Roerich Expedition was crossing Karakoram Pass, Nicholas Roerich was informed by a native guide that tall white men and women had appeared from secret entrances from the bowels of the mountains. They had been seen with torches in the dark. Travellers had even been helped by these mysterious mountain people, said one of the grooms.[20]

Madame A. David-Neel, the explorer of Tibet, writes of a Tibetan bard who was rumoured to have known the way to the 'abode of gods', somewhere in the desolate deserts and mountains of the province of Chinhai in China. Once he brought her a blue summer flower from that retreat. It was 20 degrees of frost where Madame David-Neel was at the time, and the river Dichu was frozen 6 feet deep.[21]

NORTHERN SHAMBHALA

A Shanghai newspaper in the twenties featured an article by Dr. Lao-Tsin about his journey to a utopia in Central Asia.[22] In a colourful narrative antedating James Hilton's *Lost Horizon*, the surgeon describes his hazardous trek with a Nepalese yogi to the uplands of Tibet. In a desolate mountainous region the two pilgrims found a hidden valley protected from severe northern winds and enjoying a much warmer climate than the surrounding territory. Dr. Lao-Tsin spoke of the 'Tower of Shambhala' and the laboratories which aroused his wonder. The two visitors saw great scientific achievements of the dwellers of the valley. They also watched outstanding feats in telepathy conducted over great distances. The Chinese doctor could have told much more about his stay in the valley if it were not for some promise he had given its inhabitants not to reveal all.

According to the Eastern tradition of Northern Shambhala, where now are found only salt lakes and sands, there was once a huge sea in Central Asia. This sea had an island of which nothing now remains but mountains. In that faraway epoch a great event took place: "Then with the mighty roar of swift descent from incalculable heights, surrounded by blazing masses of fire which filled the sky with shooting tongues of flame, flashed through the aerial spaces the chariot of the Sons of the Fire, the Lords of the Flame from Venus; it halted, hovering over the White Island which lay smiling in the bosom of the Gobi Sea." [23]

On the background of present-day controversy over a cosmic ship crash in Tunguska, Siberia—let us not ridicule this Sanskrit tradition.

In the folklore and songs of Tibet and Mongolia, Shambhala is exalted to a point where it assumes the form of a supreme reality. During an expedition through Central Asia Nicholas Roerich came across a white frontier post regarded as one of the three outposts of Shambhala.[22] To demonstrate how strong the belief in Shambhala was in lamahood, we will quote the words of a Tibetan monk who told Roerich that "the people of Shambhala at times emerge into the world. They meet the earthly co-workers of Shambhala. For the sake of humanity they send out precious gifts, remarkable relics".[20]

After examining the traditions of Buddhism in Tibet, Csoma de Köros (1784–1842) placed the land of Shambhala beyond Syr Daria River between 45 and 50 degrees north latitude. It is a notable fact that a seventeenth-century map (published in Antwerp, Belgium) shows the country of Shambhala.

Early Jesuit travellers in Central Asia, such as Father

Stephen Cacella, recorded the existence of an unknown domain called 'Xembala'.

Explorers Colonel N. M. Prjevalsky and Dr. A. H. Franke mention Shambhala in their works. Professor Grünwedel's translation of an ancient Tibetan book *The Path to Shambhala* is an interesting document. However, the geographical pointers seem to be purposely vague. They are of no use to anyone without a thorough familiarity with ancient and modern names of places and monasteries. Geographical indications may be confused for two reasons. Those who actually know of the colonies will never disclose where they are, so as not to disturb the humanitarian work of the Guardians. On the other hand, references to these retreats in oriental literature and folklore may sometimes seem to be conflicting because they allude to communities in diverse localities.

After having studied the subject for many years, I wrote this chapter in the Himalayas, and to me the name 'Shambhala' covers the White Island in the Gobi, hidden valleys and catacombs in Asia and other places, and a great deal more.

Lao Tse (sixth century B.C.), the founder of Taoism, searched for the abode of Hsi Wang Mu, the goddess of the west, and found it. Taoist tradition asserts that the goddess was a mortal thousands of years ago. After having become 'divine' she retreated to the Kun Lun Mountains. Chinese monks insist that there is a valley of great beauty in the range which is inaccessible to travellers without a guide. The valley is the home of Hsi Wang Mu, who presides over an assembly of genii. These may be the world's greatest scientists.

In this connection the sighting of a strange aircraft over the Karakoram (which is an extremity of the Kun Lun) by the Roerich Expedition is quite significant. The strange disc may have come from an aerodrome or spacedrome of the 'gods'.

From what has been said by now, it is clear how difficult it is to establish a contact with the dwellers of the secret communities. Yet these meetings have taken place more often than reported. The absence of records is explained by the inevitable vow of secrecy which is demanded of the visitors to these ancient colonies for a justifiable reason. The 'Mahatmas' do not wish to be disturbed by curiosity seekers, treasure hunters or sceptics, for they are the custodians of Ancient Science and the guardians of the Treasure of the Ages.

It would be appropriate to quote from one of the letters of the Mahatmas themselves inspiringly outlining the scope of their humanitarian activities: "For countless generations hath the adept builded a fane of imperishable rocks, a giant's Tower of Infinite Thought, wherein the Titan dwelt, and will yet, if need be, dwell alone, emerging from it but at the end of every cycle, to invite the elect of mankind to co-operate with him and help in his turn enlighten superstitious man." [24] Thus wrote Mahatma Koot Humi in July 1881.

The origin of these unknown communities is lost in the night of time. It is more than likely that our elders in evolution ordered the exodus from Atlantis of the people of the 'Good Law'.

All the material and spiritual achievements of Atlantis in her splendour may still be preserved in the secret colonies. Though not represented in the United Nations Organization, this tiny republic may be the only permanent state on the planet Earth and custodian of a science that is as old as the rocks. The sceptics would do well to bear in mind that messages from the Mahatmas are still preserved in state archives of certain governments.

In the folklore of Russia there is a myth of the underground city of Kitezh, where justice reigns. The Old Believers, persecuted by the Czarist government, searched for this Promised Land. "Where to find it?" asked the young. "Follow the path of Batu," answered the old, Batu Khan, the Tartar conqueror, had come from Mongolia in his westward drive. The direction meant that the utopia was to be found in Central Asia.

Another rendition of the legend pointed to Lake Sveltloyar in Russia but it has no basis because the lake bottom has been explored and nothing discovered. It seems that the tradition of Kitezh should be placed alongside with that of Northern Shambhala. The same can be said of the myth of Belovodye.

In the Journal of the Russian Geographical Society for 1903 there is an article by Korolenko entitled "The Journey of Ural Cossacks into the Belovodye Kingdom". Likewise the West

49

Siberia Geographical Society published in 1916 an account by Belosliudov, "To the History of Belovodye".

Coming from scientific bodies, both of these articles are of extreme interest. They speak of a strange tradition which was circulating among the 'Staroveri' or Old Believers in Russia. An earthly paradise existed somewhere in 'Belovodye' or 'Belogorye'—the land of the White Waters and White Mountains. Let us recall here that Northern Shambhala was founded on the White Island.

The geographical location of this phantom kingdom may be less vague than it appears at first sight. There are many salt lakes in Central Asia, some drying and covered with a white layer. The Chang Tang and Kun Lun are snow-capped.

Nicholas Roerich learned in the Altai Mountains that there was a 'secret valley' beyond the great lakes and high mountains. Many people had tried to reach Belovodye but without success, he was told. However, a few had found it and stayed there for a short time. Two men in the nineteenth century reached the utopia and resided there temporarily. They returned and described wonders about the lost colony but "of still other wonders they were not permitted to speak".[22]

This account has many points of similarity with that of Dr. Lao-Tsin, related earlier.

That the people of these secret settlements are science-conscious can be concluded from a story of Roerich about a lama who was returning to his monastery from one of the communities. The monk had met two men carrying a thoroughbred sheep in a narrow subterranean passage. The animal was required for scientific breeding in the hidden valley.

Vatican archives preserve rare reports of missionaries in the nineteenth century which affirm that in times of crises the emperors of China used to send deputations for advice to the 'Genii of the Mountains'. These documents do not show where the Chinese couriers went to, but it could only be to the Chang Tang, Kun Lun or Himalayas.

These records of Catholic missionaries (and a work by Monseigneur Delaplace, *Annales de la Propagation de la Foi*) indicate the belief of the Chinese sages in superhuman beings living in inaccessible parts of China. The chronicles describe the 'Protectors of China' as human-like in appearance but physiologically different from man.

SACRED MOUNTAINS AND LOST CITIES

Many mountains throughout the world are considered to be the abodes of 'gods'. This is especially true of India, where this chapter is written.

Hindus believe in the divine character of Nanda Devi, Kailas, Kanchenjunga and numerous other high peaks. They think the mountains are residences of the gods. What is more, it is not only the peaks that are considered sacred but the bowels of the mountains as well.

Shiva is said to have his seat on Mount Kailas (Kang Rimpoche). He is also known to have descended upon Kanchenjunga, whereas the goddess Lakshmi, on the contrary, is reputed to have ascended to heaven from the peak. In analysing these myths one forms an impression of a two-way air or space traffic that was going on in a distant epoch when gods walked among men.

Ever since mankind had risen from the state of savagery at the dawn of civilization there appeared a belief in beneficent, powerful gods. Certain localities on earth and abodes in heaven were allocated to these sky-beings. In ancient Greece Mount Parnassus and Olympus were thought to be the thrones of these gods.

According to the Mahabharata, Asuras live in the sky while Paulomas and Kalakanjas reside in Hiranyapura, the golden city, floating in space. At the same time the Asuras have subterranean palaces. Nagas and garudas, the flying creatures, likewise have underground abodes. Do these myths allegorically speak of space platforms, cosmic flights and spacedromes on earth?

The Puranas mention 'Sanakadikas'—the Ancients of Space Dimensions. These beings remain a mystery if the possibility of space travel in remote antiquity is not accepted.

Since interstellar navigation is impossible without astronomy, the statement in the Surya Siddhanta that Maya, a ruler of Atala (Atlan?), received astronomy from the sun-god, seems to indicate a cosmic source of his knowledge.

Whether the gods are Grecian, Egyptian or Indian, they invariably pose as man's benefactors, showering upon him useful knowledge and warning him in critical times.

The scriptures of India speak of Mount Meru, the centre of the world. On the one hand, it is identified with Mount Kailas in Tibet, on the other, it is said to rise 84,000 yojanas or 411,600 miles above the earth. Is Mount Kailas a gateway to space which had existed long before the last cataclysm destroyed Atlantis?

Tales of superior beings residing on certain mountains are scattered far and wide. In American Indian mythology of the Pacific north-west, Mount Shasta in California occupies a prominent place. One legend recounts the story of the Flood. It tells how an ancient hero Coyote ran to the top of Mount Shasta to save himself. The water followed him but did not reach the peak. On the only dry spot, the top of the mountain, Coyote made a fire. When the Flood subsided, Coyote brought fire to the few survivors of the cataclysm and became their culture hero.[25]

In these myths we also hear of ancient times when the Chief of the Sky-Spirits descended upon Mount Shasta with his family. Visits of the earth-people to the abodes of the Sky-People are also mentioned.

Mount Shasta myths may refer to actual incidents of the past—the Great Flood, landing of aviators or astronauts, and the establishment of underground shelters inside the mountain. Moreover, this colony may still be alive. There is evidence which supports this supposition.

After the Gold Rush days in California, in the middle of last century, prospectors reported mysterious flashes over Mount Shasta. These had sometimes taken place in clear weather, showing that they had nothing to do with lightning. Electricity could not account for the flashes because the country was not yet electrified. In more recent times cars on the roads of Mount Shasta have been known to develop ignition trouble without any apparent cause.

When a forest fire swept over Mount Shasta in 1931, a mystery fog appeared which stopped it from advancing. The demarcation line of the fire damage could be seen for many years. It went around the central zone in a perfect curve.

A curious article was featured by the *Los Angeles Times* in 1932. Its author, Edward Lanser, claimed that after interviewing residents in the Mount Shasta area, it emerged that the existence of a strange community on or in the mountain had been known for decades. The inhabitants of the phantom village were white, tall, noble-looking men with close-cropped hair and a band across their foreheads. They were dressed in white robes. Merchants said that the men used to come to their shops on rare occasions. The purchases were always paid for with gold nuggets, well in excess of the value of the goods.[26] When seen in the forest the Shastians tried to avoid contact by escaping or by instantly vanishing from sight. Strange cattle belonging to the Shasta dwellers have appeared on the slopes of the mountain. They were unlike any animals known in America. To add to the enigma, rocket-like airships have been observed over Mount Shasta territory. They were wingless and noiseless, sometimes diving into the Pacific Ocean to continue out on the sea as vessels or submarines.[27]

Is there a shelter of the Sky-People in the heart of the mountain as the old Indian legends say? Did they truly escape from a global deluge in aircraft?

Similar secret communities seem to exist in Mexico. In his book *Mysteries of Ancient South America* Harold T. Wilkins writes of an unknown people in Mexico which used to barter goods with the Indians. They were supposed to have come from a lost jungle city.

Roerich's report spoke of mysterious men and women from the mountains who bought goods in Sinkiang and paid for them with ancient gold coins. California, Mexico and Turkestan are far apart, yet the tales about the strange people seem to have many points of resemblance.

L. Taylor Hansen in *He Walked the Americas* tells of an American couple who were flying over Yucatan's jungle in their private plane many years ago. Because of fuel shortage they were forced to crash-land. In the jungle they came upon a secret Mayan city camouflaged against survey from the air.

The Mayas live in ancient splendour in complete isolation

from the outer world to preserve their hoary culture, which, no doubt, has its origin in Atlantis. The Americans pledged not to reveal the location of their city. After a long stay in Yucatan, the American couple returned to the United States with an extremely high opinion of the moral and intellectual level of the secret inhabitants of Mexico.

In the *Incidents of Travel in Central America, Chiapas and Yucatan* J. L. Stephens, noted American archaeologist, cites the story of a Spanish padre in 1838–9 who saw from the Cordillera: "A large city spread over a great space, and with turrets white and glittering in the sun. Tradition says that no white man has ever reached this city; that the inhabitants speak the Maya language, know that strangers have conquered their whole land, and murder any white man who attempts to enter their territory. They have no coin, no horses, cattle, mules, or other domestic animals."

The Spanish conquistadores recorded the Aztec tradition of hidden outposts in the jungle with vast stores of treasure and supplies. These reserve bases had become almost forgotten when the invaders landed in Mexico. Verrill writes that "because no one has ever discovered any of these 'lost cities' does not prove that they did not exist or that they may not exist at the present time".[28]

The Quechua Indians of Peru and Bolivia point to an extensive subterranean network in the Andes. Considering the outstanding engineering achievements of pre-Inca master builders, these tales could be true.

Colonel P. H. Fawcett sacrificed his life in search of a lost city which, he thought, could prove the reality of Atlantis. He claimed to have seen the ruins of such a city in South America.

The legends of lost cities, sacred mountains, hidden valleys and catacombs should be examined without any bias as some of these traditions lead to the colonies of Atlantean descendants or even of still earlier races.

CHAPTER FOUR

WHEN GODS WALKED AMONG MEN

DEMIGODS AND HISTORY

In the *Metamorphoses* of the Roman poet Ovid it is said that when the mud from the world flood became dry, the earth brought forth new and strange forms of life, though some of the old forms had survived.

Plato recorded the tradition of Egyptian priests to the effect that there had been many devastating catastrophes in the past. The sages of the Nile pointed out that, as many generations of survivors had died with no power to express themselves in writing, the memory of these cataclysms was lost.

Because of the global scope of the Atlantean disaster, many centuries had passed before volcanic activity subsided. Until land, washed away by tidal waves, was dry enough to bear vegetation, no animal or human life could exist. Atlantean survivors were scattered all over the earth. The centre of culture and the elements of civilization had perished. For lack of writing in the conditions of savagery imposed by the catastrophe, tales of a rich empire destroyed by fire and water were passed from mouth to ear. These became the origins of all myths. Handed down from one generation to another, some facts were forgotten or distorted. It was only with the rediscovery of the art of writing that legends were permanently recorded on tablets and papyri.

Folklore has immortalized divine beings who civilized mankind after the deluge. These torchbearers of culture implanted sun-worship. They became beneficent rulers who taught man astronomy, agriculture, architecture, medicine and religion. Clay tablets of Babylon speak thus of sky-descended beings: "Then came the Flood and after the Flood kingship again descended from heaven."

The chroniclers of Sumer left us their lists of kings who

ruled after the deluge. Historians had no faith in these royal listings because they contained several rulers who were marked as 'gods' or 'demigods'. Moreover, the period covered by the kings of the first dynasty after the Flood was indicated as 24,150 years. All this seemed incredible to archaeologists.

Until the twentieth century archaeology did not have a single document proving the existence of kings in Babylon earlier than the eighth dynasty. Then Sir Leonard Woolley discovered at the mount of al'Ubaid near Ur an ancient temple dedicated to the goddess Nin-Kharsag. Among the relics found was a golden bead with the name of A-anni-pad-da. Subsequently, a foundation table was detected. In cuneiform writing it confirmed the dedication of the temple by A-anni-pad-da, King of Ur, son of Mes-anni-pad-da, King of Ur.

Now Mes-anni-pad-da was the founder of the third dynasty after the Flood in the Sumerian lists of sovereigns, and until then considered merely a legendary personality. This shows how unwise it is to reject some records as fables. In this instance we see clear references to the cataclysms and the 'divine dynasties' which assisted mankind in rehabilitation.

The city of Babylon, according to Eupolemus (second century B.C.), owes its foundation to those who were saved from the catastrophe of the deluge. The kings of Sumer were supposed to be the descendents of those who were rescued from the Flood, and then sent by 'gods' to rehabilitate the human race. The first of these divine kings was Dungi, the son of goddess Ninsun.[29]

Academician V. A. Obrutchev of U.S.S.R. believed that the cataclysm survivors carried the torch of enlightenment to all the continents. This school of scientific thought defines the vanished civilization as the 'mother culture'.

The superior beings who re-civilized humanity after Atlantis, were usually deified. The Incas were worshipped as Sons of the Sun and so were the ancient Egyptian rulers. Herodotus was quite definite about Egypt having been ruled by 'gods' who lived amongst men. He recorded that Horus, who vanquished Typhon, was the last god to sit upon the throne of Egypt.

When the settings were ready for man's new act upon earth, culture heroes appeared. Dionysus, an offspring of Poseidon—

the king of Atlantis—travelled through all the world instruct-
ing the primitive peoples in agriculture and ethics.

The Turin Papyrus states that the installation of a dynasty
of demigods in Egypt took place in 9850 B.C.

Jean Bailly, eighteenth-century savant of France, raises a
logical question in his monumental work on the history of
astronomy: "What are finally all those reigns of Indian Devas
and (Persian) Peris; or those reigns of the Chinese legends;
those Tien-hoang or the Kings of Heaven, quite distinct from
the Ti-hoang, or Kings on Earth, and the Gin-hoang, the King-
men, distinctions which are in perfect accord with those of
the Greeks and Egyptians, in enumerating their dynasties of
gods, or demigods and mortals." [30]

Traditions about 'gods' and 'demigods' are universal in
scope and everlasting in time. Although superstition has often
accompanied these beliefs, they are vague memories of olden
times when men from a former super-civilization guided the
descendants of cataclysm-survivors.

THE TORCHBEARERS OF CULTURE
The Book of the Dead has a record of Thoth, the god of literature and science. His birthplace was in a far country in the
west which had a city by the sea and two active volcanoes.
One day something extraordinary happened in the land of
Thoth and the sun was darkened. This horrified even the
'gods', but the learned Thoth helped them to escape from the
menaced place to an eastern country which they reached by
crossing water. In reading this passage from the ancient
Egyptian book one cannot help thinking about Atlantis.

L. Filipoff, astronomer of the Algiers Observatory, has dis-
covered new facts in old pyramid texts (fifth to sixth dynasties).
As the god Thoth was connected with the zodiacal sign of
Cancer, the scientist concludes that the arrival of the culture-
bearer in Egypt occurred when the vernal equinox was in
Cancer or about 7256 B.C.

It is said that Hermes, who is identified with Thoth, was so
moved with compassion for a race living without law, that
he taught men science, religion, art and music, and ascended
to heaven. Hermes instructed humanity how to write down

57

their thoughts, how to observe the stars, how to play the lyre, how to cure the body and how to melt metals. Hermes or Mercury was the celestial messenger of the gods, son of Zeus and Maia. It is he who interpreted to men the wisdom of divine beings. In fact, the name Hermes means 'Interpreter' in Greek. As the grandson of Atlas, he had an Atlantean pedigree.

Mercury or Hermes was usually portrayed wearing winged sandals and hat, and carrying a caduceus—a staff with two serpents and wings as an emblem of his mission of an emissary of the heavenly gods.

Before leaving the earth and departing for the stars, Hermes bequeathed to mankind his Emerald Tables which read: "What is above is the same as that which is below, and what is below is like that which is above to accomplish the wonders of One Thing."

The discoveries of modern science in biology, atomics and astronomy demonstrate the similarity between the infinitely small and the infinitely great, and prove the truth of the Law of Hermes. The Emerald Tables contain the following paragraph: "As all things owe their existence to the will of the Only One, so all things owe their origin to the One Only Thing."

This sums up well the modern scientific views on the unity of matter. In the text of this ancient document one can also perceive hints at cosmic rays, atomic energy and its dangers.

Iamblichus (A.D. 363) and Clement of Alexandria (second century) wrote about the forty-two sacred books of Egyptian priests. The rolls were shown to Iamblichus, who was told that Thoth (Hermes) was their author. Thirty-six contained the history of all human knowledge and six treated of medicine and surgery. Some Egyptologists entertain the idea that the so-called Papyrus Ebers may be a fraction of these lost works of Hermes.

Orpheus, the son of Apollo, was another divine civilizer who brought the torch of culture to ancient Greece. Orpheus was a great seer, magician and philosopher. He taught that matter had existed from all eternity and contained in itself the principles of all existences. It is surprising to find so deep a concept at the dawn of history. It is even more astonishing to hear Orpheus speak of other worlds. In fact, he is said to have been the first to consider the probability of life in the stars.[31] It is impossible to see how Orpheus could have conceived so grand an idea as the habitability of other planets if we reject the reality of a cultural heritage from Atlantis.

It is quite probable that the Ancient Mysteries were the custodians of this arcane science. The Mysteries claimed to possess knowledge of 'celestial beings'. Virgil recorded in the fourth *Eclogue* a prophecy of their return from heavenly realms.

In India they remember an age when men could converse with gods. Was it then that the divine visitors told the Brahmins about life in the cosmos? How otherwise could the sages write in the Vedas that "there is life on other celestial bodies far from the earth"?

'AMPHIBIANS' BRING SCIENCE

The spectacular rise of Sumerians from thousands of years of barbarism to a brilliant epoch is puzzling if we discard the myths of some wonderful beings who came as civilizers.

Babylonian tradition speaks of regular visitations of the gods who taught men the arts and crafts. One of these mysterious beings was Oannes, the fish-god.

Berosus, a Chaldean priest who lived at the time of Alexander the Great, left an excellent record of the activities of Oannes and his comrades. Learned Berosus writes that in ancient Babylon people were like beasts. Then a strange creature emerged out of the Persian Gulf. Its body was similar to that of a fish but under the fish's head there was a human head. The feet were joined, forming something like a fish's tail. Yet this odd creature could speak, although described by ancient Babylonians as "an animal destitute of reason".

Oannes came out daily from the sea to give the primitive inhabitants of Mesopotamia "an insight into letters and sciences and arts of every kind". He instructed the first men of Babylon how "to construct cities, to found temples, to compile laws, and explained to them the principles of geometrical knowledge". The early Babylonians were also taught agriculture and, as Berosus says,—"in short, he instructed them in every-

59

thing which could tend to soften manners and humanize their lives".

The chronicle states that since the appearance of Oannes and "other amphibians"—"nothing material has been added by way of improvement of his instructions".

A tale about "amphibians" or "animals destitute of reason" who acted as science teachers, does not make much sense. Oannes was no god because Berosus clearly says that "his voice and language was articulate and human". Where this culture bearer had come from, is a question which can be answered only if we admit the existence of a superior civilization in former times, or else on other planets.

Berosus tells us that Oannes's head was contained within the fish's head. Is this not a good description of a space helmet within which could be seen the face of a man? Feet subjoined to the fish's tail may be a crude definition of the appearance of the lower part of a pressurized suit. How could the primitive people find words to describe these strange visitors except by a comparison with known things?

Whoever the creatures were, the facts speak for themselves as immediately after their visitations, men began to build cities, construct canals and experiment in the realm of abstract thought. It is then that art, music, religion and science were born in Babylon.

Dwellers in the Euphrates valley were beast-like before Oannes, but after him they became civilized and reached a high level of intellectual development. By the second millennium before our era, the mathematicians of Babylon were already proficient in algebra and geometry. The astronomers had exact tables in algebra and knew the position of celestial bodies at any time. And it all started with a fish-like 'god' who had come out of the waters of the Persian Gulf.

Oannes of Eridu was said to be the father of metallurgy. A hymn to him runs: "It is thou that purifiest gold and silver and mixed copper and tin." Bronze is an alloy of copper with one-tenth part of tin. It must have taken ages for man to discover that an addition of tin to copper produces a strong metal, unless the secret was handed as a gift by a superior technological civilization. Europe has had a long bronze age but hardly any copper age. Bronze articles seem to have appeared suddenly and spread evenly. Prehistoric bronze artifacts of Europe show marks of fine workmanship.

The wide distribution of bronze objects in Europe compels one to make a startling conclusion that in a distant epoch there was more traffic between the different parts of the continent than at the dawn of ancient Roman history. This hints at manufacturing skills and transport facilities in pre-history. The riddle of the bronze age is not confined to Europe alone, as in Central America bronze also came ready-made from an unknown source.

K. K. Doberer claims that Atlantean ships had sailed around Africa and reached Asia. He writes in *The Goldmakers* that between 8,000 and 10,000 B.C. a group of people landed in the Indus delta as well as at the head of the Persian Gulf. These non-Aryan and non-Semitic men founded a civilization based on the mastery of metals. The tall, black-haired strangers knew how to work gold and silver, copper and lead, tin and antimony, iron and nickel. What they knew of metals in 8000 B.C. was not learnt by the Europeans until many thousand years later.[32]

The German writer also theorises that alchemy, or transmutation of metals, was born in Atlantis. Artificially-produced gold was brought in ships from Atlantis for the exclusive use of religion. The priesthood of Sumer, India and Egypt reserved this sacred science for themselves.

Then with the introduction of alloys by the messengers from a foreign land, a technical revolution began building up a new civilization after the Great Flood.

Sumerian metal articles have been dug up in Southern Russia, Troy and Central Europe. By about 300 B.C. the superior tin-bronze culture disappeared in Sumeria mainly because of the absence of the supply of tin. Gradually prehistoric metallurgy declined and became forgotten, to be rediscovered anew many centuries later.

FROM THE LAND OF SUNRISE

Garcilasso de la Vega transmitted to us the history of the Incas. The Sun, the great parent of mankind, in token of compassion sent Manco Copac and Mama Ocllo to teach men the arts of agriculture and women the crafts of weaving and spinning. The people of Peru accepted the Children of the Sun and laid the foundations of the city of Cuzco. Another legend describes bearded white men who came from the east and imparted the blessings of civilization to the natives.

Blood tests on the tissues of five Inca mummies in the British Museum were made in 1952 by B. E. Gilbey and M. Lubran and reported to the Royal Anthropological Institute. Three out of the five mummies possessed traces of Group A, which is utterly foreign to the American Indian. None was rhesus-negative but one had the substances D and c with the absence of C and E. This combination is rare among the Indians. Further, another royal Inca mummy had the substances C, E and c, with the absence of D. This blood sample is very unique, and almost without a parallel on our earth. These overwhelming facts prove that the Inca kings could not have belonged to the original population of South America.

It should also be noted that the Spanish conquistadores heard the Inca courtiers speak a secret language which their subjects could not understand.

A similar tradition exists in Mexico, Guatemala and Yucatan where Quetzalcoatl, Kukumatz or Kukulkan is called a godman. He was a white man with a ruddy complexion and long beard. On his shoulders was a long robe of black linen with short sleeves. Toltecs, skilful craftsmen, builders, sculptors and agriculturalists followed Quetzalcoatl.

The Feathered Serpent, or Quetzalcoatl, arrived from an eastern land and opened in Mexico an era of great prosperity and progress. One version has an interesting detail as to the manner of his arrival. Quetzalcoatl is said to have landed at the spot now known as Vera Cruz in a strange, winged ship.[28] In Codex Vindobonensis he is shown descending to earth from a hole in the heavens.

When culture hero's mission was interrupted by enemies, he returned to the coast and set out for the country of Tlapallan on a raft of snakes. Another myth describes how the messenger cast himself on to a funeral pyre. His ashes then flew up and were changed into birds while his heart became the planet

Venus. Quetzalcoatl was resurrected and went to heaven as a god. Was his winged ship—a spaceship, and the funeral pyre —its fiery launching?

As civilizer, architect, agriculturist and religious leader Quetzalcoatl left behind him an unforgettable mark on the history of Mexico. He is still greatly venerated in that country.

According to Pedro de Cieza de Leon, Viracocha of the Incas was a tall white man who came from the land of dawn. He instilled kindness in the hearts of Quechua Indians and revealed to them the secrets of civilization. After completing his mission he disappeared into the sea. Viracocha's name means 'foam of the sea'. The sentiments of the Indian in regard to the legend of the white demigod have been so strong that even today some Peruvian Indians salute a friendly white stranger with the greeting—"Viracocha".

There is a considerable similarity between the legends of Quetzalcoatl and Viracocha in America, and the tradition of Oannes, the Fish-Man, in Babylon, geographically so far apart. The mythology of many races abounds in stories about gods who once trod the earth. Fanciful as the myths are, there is no doubt that some of them may be records of actual historical events.

All these apostles of civilization, descending from the sky or emerging out of the sea, plant ready-made culture among primitive tribes. Who were the founders of solar dynasties? They were the last Atlanteans who had been saved from the Great Flood in airships and spaceships as the *Epic of Gilgamesh* suggests.

The British scientist W. J. Perry believed that the Age of the Gods was largely bound up with the Children of the Sun: "The conclusion, therefore, seems forced upon us that the various groups of children of the Sun throughout the world are derived from one primordial stock." [33] That source may have been the legendary Atlantis.

In the East, India in particular, the guest is a sacred person because gods are believed to have appeared unexpectedly in olden times in the form and attire of man. To retain for themselves the favours of possible celestial visitors, the Hindus treat the guest with veneration and hospitality up to this day, even if he is only human. This tradition goes back for thousands of years to a time when gods trod the earth.

In India I had a few embarrassing moments when standing decorated with tropical garlands, men and women prostrated at my feet to pay homage to a visiting 'god'.

CHAPTER FIVE

MARKS OF A MYSTERY RACE

FOOTPRINTS AND PORTRAITS

In 1959 a shoe print was found on sandstone in the Gobi Desert, millions of years old. According to science, man was then still in the womb time. The Soviet-Chinese paleontological expedition led by Dr. Chow Ming Chen, which made the discovery, could offer no explanation of this strange find.[34]

An imprint on limestone of the Triassic period in Fisher Canyon in Pershing County, Nevada, shows a shoe-sole with faint traces of stitches. In the age of the dinosaurs there were no shoe-makers, yet the question remains—who made that shoe or sandal? Two deductions can be drawn from these artifacts: either man had appeared on this planet millions of years earlier than science supposes, or cosmic guests indeed had walked on earth in past ages. Irrespective of which conclusion is the correct one, both are equally fantastic.

A 40,000-year-old skull of a primitive man has been found in a cave at Broken Hill, Northern Rhodesia, and is preserved now in the Natural History Museum, London. It shows a neat round hole. There are no radial cracks, usually present if the injury is caused by a tusk, horn or cold weapon. It is the type of clean hole only made by a bullet. The opposite side of the skull is missing—a fact which fits this theory.[35]

Professor K. K. Flerov, Director of the Paleontological Museum of the U.S.S.R. Academy of Sciences, has the skull of an ancient bison which is so old that it makes our caveman's skull a positive newcomer. The skull is hundreds of thousands of years old. It has a similar bullet hole and scientific evidence has proved that the animal did not die of this wound. During its life the wound healed. Who and with what weapon shot at the bison in an epoch when man is presumed to have been but a man-ape? [35]

Bones of prehistoric ostriches, camels and hyenas were found in caves at Odessa, U.S.S.R., by T. G. Gritsai and I. J. Yatsko in 1960. They were about a million years old. The attention of the scientists was drawn to the fact that the bones were skilfully cut. The holes were perfectly circular, the grooves regular. Experts stated that the bones were cut with a metal tool and then polished. According to the generally-accepted scientific opinion, there were no artisans one million years ago. Whose hands carved those bones? [34]

The so-called eoliths or peculiar flints found in France, Great Britain, Germany, Russia, Egypt, Burma and Australia, in beds ranging from Eocene to post-glacial period, may belong to the same class of artifacts. While most scientists oppose the theory of their artificial origin, more evidence is needed to prove that they are natural stones formed by glaciers or sea waves.

The footprints in Central Asia and Nevada are not the only marks of a mystery race. In the rock paintings of Africa and Australia are perpetuated the images of these men. Among the Tassili frescoes discovered by Professor Henri Lhote in Sahara is the 'great Martian god of Jabbaren'. It depicts men in what appear to be space suits. The age of the rock paintings is estimated at 8,000–10,000 years. Whose portraits are they?

Puzzling portrait galleries exist in the caves of the Kimberley Ranges in Western Australia. The aborigines say they were made by another race. The technique of artwork and the employment of a blue pigment not used by the aborigines, attributes the authorship of these drawings to a people of non-Australian origin. The Kimberley rock paintings portray figures with peculiar head-dress or halos but no mouths. In the land of bare-footed natives, the figures are painted with sandals on their feet.

These 'Wandjina' pictures are supposed to represent the first men. It should be noted here that they are depicted with three or seven fingers and toes. The Wandjina are connected with the Rainbow Serpent paintings in the Kimberleys. The Rainbow Serpent is the term for 'Dreamtime' or the prehistoric age.

There is a remarkable affinity between the Tassili rock paintings and those of the Kimberleys. The creatures without mouths may be beings in space helmets. Numerous theories have been advanced to explain the Mouthless Ones, yet none is satisfactory.

CUBES, SPHERES AND LINES

The Kutb Minar pillar in Delhi, India, is a riddle. This iron shaft is about 26 feet 3 inches high and its thickness is such that it can be encircled by the two arms of a standing man. The column weighs 2 tons. The inscription at its base says: "Whilst I stand, shall the Hindu Kingdom endure."

The iron of which the Kutb Minar pillar is made does not rust. To produce such non-corrosive iron is a task even for our modern technology equipped with electric furnaces. The secret of ancient artificers who had produced this wonderful metal, of which the column was constructed 1,500 years ago, is lost in the night of time.

In 1885 a steel cube was found in a block of coal at the foundry of Isidore Braun of Vöcklabruck, Austria. The coal came from the Wolfsegg mine near Schwanenstadt. Herr Braun's son donated this remarkable object to the Linz Museum. However, only a cast is preserved at the museum at present as the original has been lost. The cube was described in contemporary journals, such as *Nature* (London, November 1886), *L'Astronomie* (Paris 1886) and others. Its two opposite sides are rounded so that the dimensions between the rounded faces are 67 millimetres by 47 millimetres. A deep incision runs all round the cube near its centre. Its weight is 785 grams (26 ounces) and in composition it resembles a hard nickel-carbon steel. The sulphur content is far too low for it to be any kind of natural pyrites.

The metal piece was encrusted in a block of coal of the Tertiary epoch, tens of millions of years old. Some scientists considered it to be a fossil meteorite. Others, because of its geometrical form and the indentation, thought the object was artificial in origin, or man-made. But, according to science, man was then non-existent on this planet. The artifact still remains unexplained.[36]

A meteorite of unusual shape, found at Eton, Colorado, and studied by the meteorics expert, H. H. Nininger, is another mystery. Its chemical composition is copper, zinc and lead, or brass which is an artificial alloy and not a natural substance. The meteorite is not 'space garbage', because it fell in 1931.

In the sixteenth century the Spaniards found a 7-inch iron nail solidly encrusted into rock in a Peruvian mine. It can safely be assumed that it was tens of thousands of years old. In a country where iron was unknown until recent time, this was truly a surprising discovery, and it is no wonder that the curious nail was proudly displayed in the study of Francisco de Toledo, the viceroy of Peru.

On the barren tablelands near Nasca, Peru, there exist huge figures and lines many miles long, laid out on the ground by means of rocks. It was in an aerial survey that the patterns were discovered. These geometrical configurations on the ground have remained a mystery ever since their discovery. "How were they made so perfect without being seen in proper perspective?", asks J. Alden Mason in *The Ancient Civilization of Peru*. Did the Nasca lines serve as beacons for ancient aircraft?

Among the possible traces left by Atlantis could be hundreds of those strange globes which are found in the jungles of south-western Costa Rica, Guatemala and Mexico. These stone balls are finely polished, and range from a few inches to 8 feet in diameter. These spheres of volcanic rock, some weighing many tons, are perfectly shaped. What is puzzling is the absence of any tools by means of which they could have been made on the sites of the finds. The rock of which the globes are made, is located at a considerable distance. Who made these mystery globes? To what epoch do they belong? How were they transported from afar and placed on tops of mountains and for what purpose? These are the problems which archaeology is trying to solve.

Some of the balls are arranged in triangular formations suggesting some astronomical or religious symbolism. It is thought that the civilization which manufactured these spheres must have been highly advanced.[37]

A number of mysterious toys found near Vera Cruz, Mexico, represent alligator-like animals on four wheels. This is strange as the American Indian never had the wheel. Cars were unknown in the Americas before the Spanish Conquest. Carbon datings of these wheeled toys show that they are from 1,200 to 2,000 years old. The question still remains—why did not the Mayas use vehicles if their children played with the wheeled toys. After all, our kids play with toy cars because the grown-ups drive automobiles.

Few anthropologists, if any, would entertain the idea of co-existence of prehistoric animals with a civilized race of men. However, Professor Denis Saurat of France has recognized the heads of toxodons in the ornaments of the calendar of Tiahuanaco. In his opinion, the simultaneous existence of the toxodons and the builders is incontestable.[38]

In 1924 the Doheny Archaeological Expedition discovered a rock painting in the Hava Supai Canyon, North Arizona. The image resembles the figure of a standing tyrannosaurus. However, it is thought that the monster died out millions of years ago, long before the advent of man.

This prehistoric painting suggests that the primitive artist was a contemporary of the tyrannosaurus. It is reasonable to conclude that the time of the extinction of this monster has to be stretched forward, or else the date of man's birth on earth should be moved backward.

A rock carving in the Big Sandy River in Oregon can be identified as a stegosaurus—another creature which had supposedly disappeared before the arrival of *homo sapiens*.

If an explorer came across an elephant in the jungles of Central America today, he would probably have the shock of his life. Yet elephants must have lived there in a comparatively recent past. Among the relics of the Cocle culture in Panama is an image of an elephant with a trunk, big leaf-like ears and a load strapped upon its back. This sculpture is not the only one of its kind in that part of the world.[28] In Copan, Honduras, elephants with men riding on their backs are depicted on a stone monument. However, some archaeologists—whose scepticism is sometimes much greater than their common sense— identified them as parrots. On Marcahuasi plateau near Lima, Peru, huge rock carvings of elephants considered extinct in America for 7,000 years, have likewise been discovered. The images of these elephants were so definite that Dr Daniel Ruzo, who made the discovery, did not class them as parrots. In this

69

rock gallery Ruzo found images of camels, horses and cows, none of which were present in the Americas at the time of Columbus. The most ancient character of this rock art exhibition is beyond doubt.

The 'elephant controversy' can not continue any longer because the fossilized remains of an early man with the bones of an extinct elephant have been discovered by Helmut de Terra at Tepexpan, Mexico. According to a Carbon-14 test, they lived about 9300 B.C., or some 250 years after the traditional date of the sinking of Atlantis. What science may still contest is the hoary age of some of the elephant ornaments and sculptures in Central and South America.

The Cocle pottery designs represent a flying lizard which looks almost like the extinct pterodactyl. It is significant that creatures of a prehistoric type are painted along with the recognizable animals.[28]

Two extremely old cities have been uncovered in the Nasca district near Pisco, Peru. Among the archaeological finds from a civilization immeasurably more ancient than the pre-Incan culture, strange vessels were found by Professor Julio Tello about 1920. Jugs depict a five-toed llama. The animals now have two toes only but an early evolutionary stage they had five, as our cattle once did. What is more, these llamas with five toes are not imaginary creatures because their skeletons have actually been excavated in the same area. An interesting conclusion can be drawn from this fact—a cultured people lived in South America in a very remote epoch when llamas still had five toes.[28,39]

In the State Hermitage Museum, Leningrad, there is a golden buckle of Scythian origin which contains an image of the sabre-tooth tiger, extinct since the end of the Ice Age.

On Malta there is a mysterious track, cut in rock, with junctions and sidings like a railway. The grooves run by the side of a narrow strip of rock where no animals, dragging a cart, could pass. Neither are there any hoof marks or traces of footsteps between the deep grooves. At another point the track leaves the seashore and stretches under water for some distance. The purpose of so strange an archaeological find is undefined, especially of such antiquity as 9,000 years.

The Scientific American (7–298, June 1851) reported that in a blast near Dorchester, Massachusetts, a bell-shaped vessel of an unknown metal, with floral designs inlaid with silver, was found embedded in solid rock.

These puzzles of science may one day compel our savants to extend the historical horizon for many thousand years.

CHAPTER SIX

EARLY SCIENCE—A LEGACY

SCIENCE BEFORE THE AGE OF SCIENCE

Rock paintings in Canchal de Mahoma and Abri de las Viñas, Spain show mysterious markings. A mammoth ivory artifact from Gontzi, Ukraine dating to the Ice Age, contains a peculiar notation. Thousands of these engraved or painted markings are scattered throughout Europe. They have perplexed archaeologists and anthropologists for a long time.

Alexander Marshack in a magazine article in *Science* has successfully demonstrated that these complex notations represent accurate lunar observations made thousands of years before the dawn of history. The data prompted Alexander Marshack to ask for a reappraisal of views on prehistory: "The questions raised by this evidence of lunar notation in the Upper Paleolithic period are many and important. They entail a re-evaluation of the origins of human culture, including the origins of art, symbol, religion, rite and astronomy, and of the intellectual skills that were available for the beginnings of agriculture." [40]

These notational sequences and markings, dating from the Upper Paleolithic, extend backward in an unbroken line from the Mesolithic Azilian to the Magdalenian and Aurignacian cultures. Then Marshack quite correctly concludes that: "The combined evidence of a lunar and an occasional lunar-solar lore in the early agricultural civilizations, which was spread across the land mass of Eurasia, branched into Africa, and was practised by different peoples speaking different languages, raises the question as to whether an earlier, basic astronomical skill and tradition existed." [40]

The *Popol Vuh* of Guatemala contains a record of the achievements of primordial men and says that: "They contemplated in turn the arch of heaven and the round face of the earth. Great was their wisdom." The sacred book adds that they could "also see the large and the small in the sky and on earth."

It is odd but true that at the dawn of civilization scientific knowledge was occasionally well above the intellectual level of the times. This can be accounted for by a heritage from an archaic, pre-deluge world. Traces of this 'master culture' remained after the global disaster. This is the reason why a study of ancient sources is pursued in this chapter. The farther we go down into the past, the closer we are to that lost civilization.

Professor Frederick Soddy wrote in 1909 that atomic energy was the motive power behind antediluvian technology. "A race which could transmute matter," he said, "would have little need to earn its bread by the sweat of its brow. Such a race could transform a desert continent, thaw the frozen poles, and make the whole world one smiling Garden of Eden." [17]

In Moscow the author heard of a biography of Albert Einstein in which the founder of the Theory of Relativity expresses a similar idea that nuclear power was merely rediscovered. It is said that the editor of the manuscript decided to abstain from publishing this statement made by Einstein shortly before his death, on the ground that "the old man must have lost his mind".

Soddy saw a calamity in the past when mankind misjudged the positions of Nature and man. After this mistake the whole world was plunged into a primitive state. Then humanity again began its upward toilsome journey through the ages. "The legend of the Fall of Man possibly may indeed be the story of such a past calamity," alleged Professor Soddy, Nobel Prize winner.

There is an inexplicable affinity between the origins of cultures of remote antiquity. It can not be explained successfully by the borrowing of some peoples from others because of the vast geographical distances separating them.

A certain unknown world must be sought beyond the barriers of history. That world must have given the first impetus to all the succeeding civilizations. There is no doubt that the ancient Egyptians, Babylonians, Greeks and Romans were the

73

teachers of our modern world. But who had been the 'teachers of teachers'—of Egypt, Babylon, Greece? The Atlanteans, tradition replies. These were the reflections and conclusions of Valery Briusov, the Russian pioneer in Atlantology.

While it is well known that human progress is an evolutionary process, a portion of our accomplishments in the early stages of the present cycle may be nothing else but old knowledge passed on to generations of cataclysm survivors. Not all of the scientific achievements of the ancients were a legacy from Atlantis. Human growth, from the post-cataclysmic era of barbarism to the culture of Egypt and Sumer, was a result of natural social factors. However, while some of the discoveries of early man could have been landmarks in progress, others might have been but re-discoveries stimulated by tales of a Golden Age and its wonders.

It would be difficult to draw a line of demarcation between the products of human intelligence and the heritage from a prehistoric era. The fact remains that some of the scientific achievements of man in prehistory can not be defined as creations of his mind because economic and social conditions were not ripe for them. In this 'premature progress' are included ancient airships, X-ray and astronomical discoveries made without a telescope.

When Cortes invaded Mexico in 1520 his calendar was ten days behind that of the Aztecs and the actual astronomical time. Historically speaking, astronomy of the Old World was behind that of the New.

Incredible as it sounds in this twentieth century, the Mayan calendar was more accurate than ours because it offers the best approximation to the sidereally determined absolute year as can be seen from these figures:

Sidereal reckoning	365·242,198 days in a year
Mayan calendar	365·242,129 days in a year
Gregorian calendar	365·242,500 days in a year

What is more, in the complex chronology of the Mayas similar dates appear only once every 256 years. It goes without saying that their calendar was superior to the one we use today.

According to Egerton Sykes: "The key factor is the realization that the Maya arrived on the mainland complete with a knowledge of writing, of mathematics, of astronomy, of architecture, of medicine, and with a calendrical system which was more accurate than that used in Europe until the eighteenth century. The usual assumption that they had picked up in a hundred years or less the knowledge which it took the Western World two thousand or more years to acquire seems to me to be unrelated either to historical precedent or to common sense." [41] What was the origin of this imported culture?

Cottie A. Burland, formerly of the British Museum, reported to the International Congress of Americanists held in Paris in 1956 that Stela I, El Castillo, Santa Lucia Cotzumahualpa depicted a transit of Venus over the disc of the sun on 25 November 416. The accuracy of ancient Guatemalan astronomers is truly astonishing because it takes centuries to develop an exact science. From what source did the Central American priests derive their scientific tradition?

Aztecs had a knowledge of the regulation of traffic as well as of census taking. Incas had an effective water supply and sewage system, and the best highways in antiquity. Toltecs had building projects covering four hundred years. At present, no nation in the world, socialist or capitalist, has any planning for centuries.

It is no exaggeration to say that ancient Peruvians wove textiles far finer than is possible on any modern loom. Ornaments of platinum have been discovered on the coast of Ecuador. This little fact raised a big question—how could American Indians produce a temperature of about 1770 degrees centigrade thousands of years ago? Europe achieved this but two centuries ago.[42]

In *The Shadow of Atlantis* Braghine describes a strange object found in Esmeralda, on the northern shore of Ecuador, among many other articles of great age. In the collection of Ernesto Franco there was a green-black obsidian mirror, about 2 inches in diameter, in the shape of a convex lens. It was so precise that the reflection of the face showed the tiniest hairs. But optics requires a mastery of mathematics and an advanced technology. Where was the mirror made?

In the Museum of the American Indian, Heye Foundation, in New York are displayed tiny beads of the Manabis. Many are elaborately engraved or chased, some welded together and pierced. These minute objects, smaller than the head of a pin, look like natural grains of gold. No jeweller without a lens could have worked on these little particles.

In the Andes, south of Lima, Peru, in the Bay of Pisco, conquistadores of the sixteenth century found "the miraculous sign of the Three Crosses", which actually looks more like the trident of Neptune with branches. This engraving in rock is 810 feet high and can be seen from a distance of $12\frac{1}{2}$ miles.

The purpose and meaning of this 'Chandelier of the Andes' have remained obscure until Beltran Garcia, the Spanish scientist and direct descendant of Garcilaso de la Vega, offered his theory. He believes that the trident in rock was used by the Incas, or their predecessors, as a gigantic seismograph. In his opinion, it was a pendulum with pulleys and cords to register earthquakes not only in Peru but in the whole world. This explanation may be much nearer the truth than the one brought by the conquistadores. They thought the Sign of the Three Crosses was carved by God to thank the Christians for the conquest of the Americas.[43]

In spite of a high form of civilization the Incas had no writing, which is unprecedented in history because writing and literature are marks of cultural maturity. Instead of letters and words they had quipu—a complicated system of coloured strings with knots that served as mnemonic aids and recording devices. This peculiar system of pre-Inca origin was used in accounting and statistics as well as literature, where loops and knots reminded the story-teller of the sequence of the tale. These mnemonics can be viewed as an echo from a lost technology which used electronic computers. After the disappearance of manufacturing centres which produced this equipment, the survivors of Atlantean cataclysm in South America might have adopted a simple method of recording by

76

means of quipu—a mere caricature of their previous calculators and registers.

Scientific riddles such as the quipu are not confined to one continent or nation. Let us cross the Pacific Ocean and survey China.

Chinese historians never tried to please sovereigns at the expense of truth. They preferred execution to false recording of history, as happened to historiographers of Chi in 547 B.C. This is the reason why the chronicles of China should be taken very seriously even if they describe seemingly fabulous things.

Did ancient Chinese have the X-ray? The question may seem absurd in the extreme, yet Emperor Tsin Shi (259–210 B.C.) did have a mirror which "would illuminate the bones of the body". The mirror was located in the palace at Hien-Yang in Shensi in 206 B.C., and contemporary writings represent it as follows: "It was a rectangular mirror 4 feet wide, 5 feet 9 inches high, brilliant both on its outer and inner sides. When a man stood straight before it to see his reflection, his image appeared reversed. When someone placed his hand on his heart, he observed his five viscera placed side by side and not impeded by any obstacle. When a man had a hidden malady within his organs, he could recognize the seat of his complaint by looking into this mirror and laying his hands on his heart." [44]

About two hundred and fifty years before Emperor Tsin Shi, Jivaka, a celebrated physician of ancient India, possessed a marvellous gem which had the power of Roentgen rays to penetrate the human body. An historical record states that "when placed before an invalid, it illuminated his body as a lamp lights up all objects in a house, and so revealed the nature of his malady".[44] Where did Tsin Shi and Jivaka get the knowledge which was 2,200 to 2,500 years ahead of that of their contemporaries?

In the *Sactaya Grantham*, which belongs to the Vedas of India, there are directions for vaccination and description of its effects. How did the Brahmins make this discovery in biology some 4,000 years before Jenner?

It is strange to read of X-ray in the days of Gautama the Buddha and of vaccination 2,000 years before Jesus Christ. It

77

is stranger still to find astounding astronomical facts in texts of ancient Babylonian origin.

Babylonians knew of the 'horns of Venus'.[45] They wrote of the crescent of the planet. Since Venus is nearer to the sun than the earth, it shows phases like the moon. But the 'horns of Venus' are visible to the naked eye. The burning question is —how could ancient Babylonian priests watch the phases of Venus without a telescope? They were also aware of Jupiter's four larger moons—Io, Europa, Ganymede and Callisto.[31] Till the invention of the telescope by Galileo mankind had known nothing of these satellites. Strictly speaking, Babylonians should have had no knowledge about them, either.

There are only two explanations for these astronomical observations of the phases of Venus and the four major moons of Jupiter conducted in antiquity. The first theory that the priests of Babylon had a telescope sounds somewhat far-fetched and most scientific opinion does not even entertain it as a probability. However, the British Museum has a remark-able piece of rock crystal, oval in shape and ground to a plano-convex form. It was discovered by Sir A. Henry Layard during the excavations of Sargon's palace at Nineveh. Sir David Brewster suggested that the crystal disc was a lens but most scientists rejected his theory.[46]

The second hypothesis is that in the course of many genera-tions the priests of Chaldea and Sumer had preserved the elements of antediluvian astronomy. It must be borne in mind that the sages of Babylon were not only priests but scientists as well. Their astronomy was closely linked with religion and reserved exclusively for the elect priesthood.

The ancient Egyptians had a special hieroglyphic for a million. Not until Descartes and Leibnitz in the seventeenth century did the modern world gain any conception of millions in mathematics. Yet ancient Babylonian mathematicians man-ipulated large numbers by means of reckoning tables thousands of years ago. In their libraries they could have had tablets with information on scientific matters from a bygone age. If this supposition is correct, then it is clear how they had found out about the phases of Venus and the moons of Jupiter.

The Aztecs knew about the globular shape of the planets

and played a ball game to imitate the gods who hurled stellar bodies across the heavens.

The African Dogons, who have a theocratic system and old traditions, know of the dark companion of Sirius situated at a distance of almost nine light-years from the earth, and visible only through a telescope. Likewise, the Mediterranean people possess the knowledge of Pleiades beyond the seventh invisible to the naked eye. Are these folk memories from a vanished science?

In the study of early astronomy the accuracy of the ancients in measuring the parallax of the sun has always been a riddle because this could not be computed with the instruments then in use.[30]

The *Huai Nan Tzu* book (*c.* 120 B.C.) as well as the *Lun Heng* of Wang Chhung (A.D. 82) outline the centripetal cosmogony in which 'whirlpools' solidify worlds out of primary matter. These writings of ancient China give a preview of modern ideas on the formation of galaxies.

Thus we are faced with two alternatives—either to admit the existence of superior astronomical instruments in antiquity, or to assume that the priests of Babylon, Egypt or India were the custodians of a prehistoric science at least ten thousand years old.

FROM PHILOSOPHY TO ATOMICS

By what means had the sages of the ancient world known certain scientific facts well ahead of the people of the day? Allowance is made for brilliant philosophic speculation in olden times, but often it appears to be positive knowledge rather than vague speculation.

Anaximenes, about two and a half thousand years ago, was aware not only of the remoteness of the stars but also of their "non-luminous companions". It is only in the past few years that astronomy has obtained data on planets in other solar systems.

Anaxagoras (500–428 B.C.) wrote likewise about "other earths which produce the necessary sustenance for inhabitants". Even a century or two ago this brilliant thought of an ancient Greek would have been frowned upon by the Church

79

and questioned by the academies. Does this not prove that the philosophers of Ancient Greece had, in some inexplicable way, been closer to truth than Western Europe but a few generations ago?

Democritus (460–361 B.C.) correctly explained the Milky Way as an immense multitude of distant stars scattered in space. Our science reached this conclusion less than two hundred years ago. Was it philosophic deduction or hints from the guardians of the Wisdom of the Ages that projected the minds of these Greeks into the distant future? Like a member of a present-day academy of sciences Democritus says: "In reality there is nothing but atoms and space."

North-east of Athens, on the main highway, there is a spot where Democritus once worked, now appropriately marked 'Democritus Nuclear Research Laboratory'.

Democritus was instructed in his youth by the magi left by Xerxes in Abdera. Sextus Empiricus (early third century) writes that Democritus learned about the atomic theory from ancient tradition, particularly from Moschus the Phoenician, who had even a more correct concept of the atom as he considered it divisible. According to Seneca, Democritus "knew that there are more planets than we are able to discover with our eyes". Where did Democritus receive astronomical knowledge that was centuries ahead or, perhaps, behind his historical epoch?

Democritus postulated that the sun is of immense size, and that the markings on the moon are formed by shadows of high mountains and deep valleys. He held that worlds are constantly born and destroyed in infinite space. The stars are suns, claimed Democritus. Some of them are larger than our own, added Simplicious in the sixth century of our era. Other philosophers pointed at the enormous distances which separate our world from the stars.

Pythagoras (c. 530 B.C.) deduced that the earth is a sphere and Aristarchus of Samos (310–230 B.C.) insisted that it revolves around the sun.

Eratosthenes (276–195 B.C.), curator of the Alexandrian Library, calculated the terrestrial circumference with a slight error of 225 miles. Chaldeans, according to Achilles Tatius,

The zodiac of Denderah (Egypt) begins, oddly enough, with the sign of Leo at the vernal equinox. It covers the period 10950–8800 B.C. when, according to Plato, Atlantis was submerged. (*Photo: Agence Giraudon*)

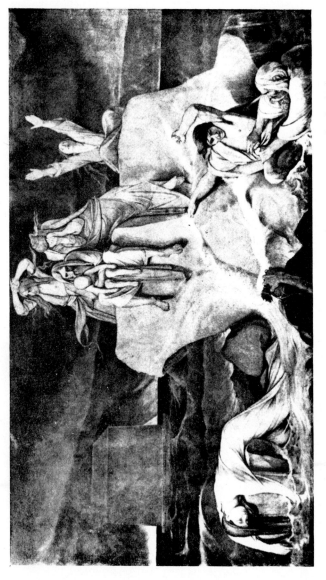

Myths. legends, and religious writings from many lands tell of a great flood which occurred in the distant past. Bruni's picture of *The Deluge* is in the cathedral of St

This puzzling bas-relief of the Maya period on a tomb in Palenque (Mexico) appears to show a pilot at the controls of an aeroplane or spaceship. (Photo: Noir et Blanc, Paris)

Quetzalcoatl: is he the messenger of the gods who brought Maya civilization to the earth, or an astronaut in his space helmet? (*Photo:* Jean Bottin)

The print of a shoe found in a limestone bed in Nevada dating from a period before the coming of man. (*Photo:* James Churchward)

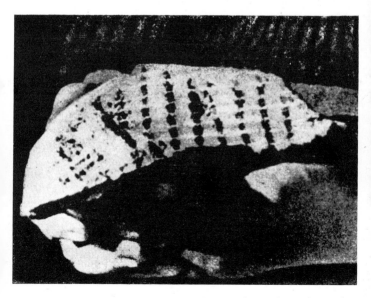

What being can have left the print of this ribbed sole in the sandstone of the Gobi desert millions of years ago? (*Photo:* Smena, USSR)

"Martians", a fresco painted about 9,000 years ago on a rock in Tassili (Sahara). (*Photo:* M. Hetier)

"The Mouthless Ones", a prehistoric painting found in the Kimberley region of Australia. Astronauts in spacesuits? (*Photo:* Mitchell Library)

The Conquisitadors discovered this "Candlestick of the Andes" in the sixteenth century; according to Beltran García it could be a huge seismograph made at a pre-Inca period of civilization. (*Photo:* Robert Charroux)

Eleven index fingers and three words chanted in unison lift this granite block weighing over a hundredweight. Is this an example of levitation? (*Photo: Illustrated Weekly of India*)

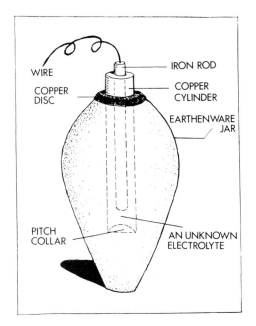

This electric cell invented in ancient Babylon proves that electricity was known to antiquity. (Author's diagram)

Fragments of a mechanical model of the solar system, Greece, 65 B.C. (*Photo:* Greek National Archaeological Museum)

The oldest map of America (1520)—attributed to Piri Reis—showing ice-free Antarctica, parts of which remained unknown up to 1957. (*Photo:* Turkish Historical Society)

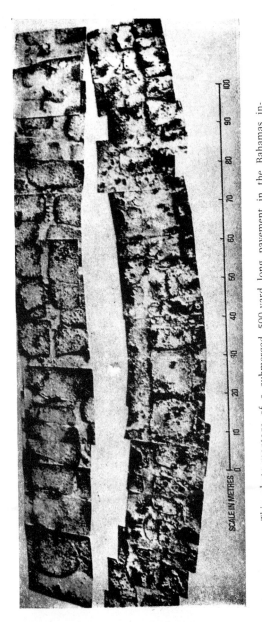

This photo-montage of a submerged 500-yard long pavement in the Bahamas indicates the size of the massive stone blocks. (*Photo: Muse News*, Museum of Science.
Miami)

SCALE IN METRES

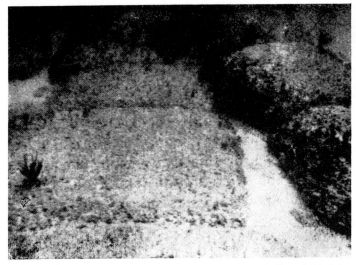

An underwater pavement of huge stone slabs discovered off north Bimini in the Bahamas. (*Photo: Muse News*, Museum of Science, Miami)

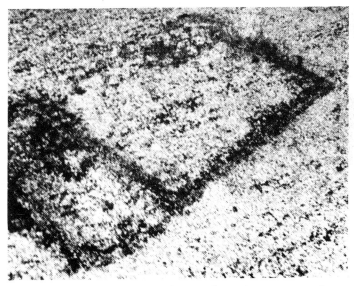

Photograph of the foundations of a 100 by 75-foot structure of an unknown civilization at the bottom of the sea off Andros Island in the Bahamas. (*Photo: Muse News*, Museum of Science, Miami)

There are many Chinese folk tales about prehistoric flight. (*Photo: China Reconstructs*, Peking, August 1961)

Ki-Kung-Shi experimented with his "Flying Chariot" in 1766 B.C.

奇肱國

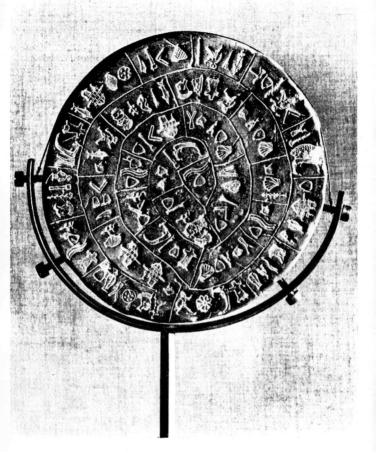

This ceramic disc with its undeciphered hieroglyphs was found at Phaistos (Crete) beside a Minoan tablet, and must thus be 3,700 years old. But as the disc is made from a clay not found in Crete, it may date back to a civilization which disappeared even earlier. (*Photo: Mme. Hassia*)

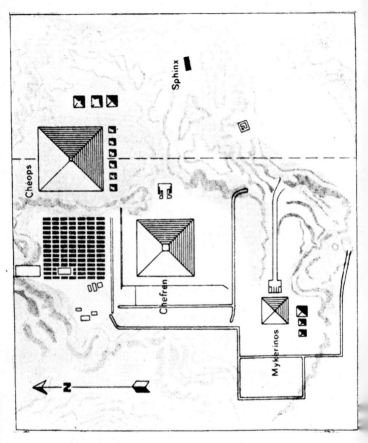

The answer to the puzzle of the location of the ancient treasure buried at Gizeh perhaps lies in the orientation of the Sphinx and Pyramids, or in their geometrical proportions. (Author's diagram)

had also measured the earth with a result which was not very far from that of Eratosthenes.

Opinions of Philosophers, attributed to Plutarch, gives the distance from the earth to the sun as 804 million stadia. This is almost the figure accepted by our astronomy, provided our estimation of the ancient stadium is correct. Did the astronomers of antiquity possess precision instruments? If not, how did they make so many wonderful guesses?

Empedocles (494–34 B.C.) argued that light required time to travel. He also had a concept of the mutation of the species. Lucretius (96–55 B.C.) was aware of the uniform speed of falling bodies in a vacuum. In the poem, "On Nature" he draws a picture of the struggle for existence, centuries before Darwin, Pythagoras, long before Newton, knew about the law of the force of attraction.

Anaximander (early sixth century B.C.) postulated that all the species of animal life had evolved from a common stock.

Instances of ancient philosophers speaking the language of our century are comparatively rare. Yet there is enough evidence to conclude that, in some respects, the thinkers of the classic world were intellectual giants compared with the scholastics of the Middle Ages.

History tells us that Archimedes constructed a planetarium in the third century before our era. The National Archaeological Museum of Greece has a remarkable relic. It was found by fishermen in the Mediterranean in 1900 but remained a mystery till 1959 when Dr Derek Price, a Cambridge scientist, identified the ancient gadget as a working model of the solar system. It is a precise mechanical model of the earth, sun, moon and planets, fashioned by some unknown craftsman about 65 B.C. This device has an intricate and precise set of gears, turned by a small crank keeping every heavenly body in proper position. The model is too delicate to touch but the gears and wheels can still be made out. Dr Price stated in 1959 that "finding a thing like this is like finding a jet plane in the tomb of King Tut".[47]

Cicero writes about a similar celestial sphere displayed in the Temple of Virtue at Rome. He stresses its ancient origin, attributing its invention to Thales of Miletus in the sixth century before our era.

Two thousand years ago the city of Syracuse in Sicily had a planetarium in which the stars were moved by hydraulic power.

Many ancient Greek thinkers went so far as to suggest life on other planets. Metrodotus of Lampsacus (third century B.C.) said that to call the earth the only populated world in the infinite reaches of space was just as unwise as to assert that there was only one ear of grain growing in a vast field.

One is astonished at this speculation, if not knowledge, about life on other planets at a time when there was no telescope and all the scientific wizardry of today. Were these philosophers ages ahead of their fellow men because of their high intelligence alone, or did they also have access to a science from a vanished civilization?

PUNDITS, STARS AND EVOLUTION

For centuries the Brahmins have zealously guarded the astronomical table of *Surya Siddhanta*. In this textbook on the astronomy of ancient India the earth's diameter was computed to be 7,840 miles. The distance of the earth to the moon was calculated at 253,000 miles. The figure accepted by modern astronomy for the equatorial diameter of our planet is 7,926·7 miles, and the maximum distance to the moon is known to be 252,710 miles. From these figures it can be seen how remarkable was the accuracy of the ancient astronomers of India, especially at a time when Europeans were suffering from a 'flat-earth' complex. The date of the *Surya Siddhanta*'s last compilation is about A.D. 1000, yet some Hindus believe that earlier editions were in existence about 3000 B.C. If so, the book is all the more puzzling.

In the Sanskrit texts of Manu we find ideas of evolution in India antedating Lamarck and Darwin by thousands of years: "The first germ of life was developed by water and heat. Man will traverse the universe, gradually ascending and passing through the rocks, the plants, the worms, insects, fish, serpents, tortoises, wild animals, cattle, and higher animals.

These are the transformations declared, from the plant to Brahma, which have to take place in his world."

Is this ancient version of evolution a deep thought from the mind of a sage, or a gift from the archaic treasury guarded by initiated priests of India?

Hindu cosmology estimates the duration of the solar system in millions of years. 'Kalpa' or the Day of Brahma—the life span of our world—is supposed to take 4,320 million years. The present age of the earth, obtained by the argon-dating method is 5,000 million years. Though modern science and Brahmin tradition do not entirely agree on the period of solar evolution, the cosmic chronology of India is certainly impressive because it deals with thousands of million years as science.

The Druses of Lebanon have a belief that the world was 3,430 million years old at the time of divine Hakim. The Metternich Stele of Egypt alludes to the 'Boat of Millions of years' in which the god Ra sails. These are clear indications that the ancients thought the universe was very ancient. Their speculations were certainly much more sensible and scientific than the conclusions of our nineteenth-century ancestors about the earth being but a few thousand years old. The source of this arcane science is hidden in the depths of time.

The pundits of India also wrote about the infinitely small in such books as the *Surya Siddhanta* or *Brihath Sathaka*. In olden times they divided the day into sixty kala or ghatika, each equal to twenty-four minutes, in turn subdivided into sixty vikala, each equivalent to twenty-four seconds. Then followed a sixty-fold division of vikala into para, tatpara, vitatpara, ima and kasha. After this split-up of time the Brahmins arrived at the smallest unit of kashta, which is equal to approximately 0·00000003 second (a three-hundred millionth of a second). Needless to say, without precision instruments, 'kashta'—as a fraction of the micro second, is absolutely meaningless. We are inclined to conclude that this measurement of time is merely a tradition preserved by the pundits from an advanced technological civilization probably familiar with nuclear physics. In fact, the author made a startling discovery during his stay in India. The 'kashta'

$(3 \times 10^{-8}$ second) is surprisingly close to the life-spans of certain mesons and hyperons!

Ancient Greeks had a curious myth. Atlas who supported pillars resting in the sea "beyond the most western horizon" had a daughter Electra. Other versions name the god Oceanus as her parent. Electra means 'bright one' in Greek. It also means 'amber' which produces electricity by friction. As Atlas is generally identified with Atlantis, can we not read in this myth the existence of electricity in Atlantis?

On the eve of World War II Wilhelm König, a German engineer and archaeologist in Iraq, made a remarkable find. During excavation work near Baghdad he accidentally discovered a Parthian village. A number of peculiar vases were found there. They reminded König of batteries of primary cells. This is what they looked like—in a pot or jar was a cylinder of sheet copper, inserted within the cylinder was an iron rod which presumably acted as an electrode. The edges of the copper cylinder were soldered with a 60:40 lead-tin alloy. The rod was held by an asphalt stopper. A copper disc was crimped into the bottom of the cylinder. Bitumen was used for insulation. The space between the walls of the copper cylinder and the iron rod was filled with some electrolyte. Because of the age of this battery Wilhelm König found no trace of the chemical.

The famous scientist Willy Ley became interested in this find and requested the General Electric Company at Pittsfield, Massachusetts, to construct a replica with the idea of testing the cell, if it was one. The General Electric Laboratory made a duplicate of the battery and filled it with copper sulphate instead of the electrolyte, which is unknown—and it worked.[48]

Archaeologists have also discovered electroplated materials 4,000 years old in the same general area where the cells were found.

The copper articles discovered at Chan-Chan in the Chimu district, Peru are plated with gold. Other ornaments, masks and beads are silver plated. Then there are a number of silver objects which are gold plated. The American author and archaeologist Verrill remarks that "so perfectly and evenly is the plating done that any one examining them would declare that they were electro-plated if their origin were not known".[28]

The tomb of the Chinese general Chow Chu (A.D. 265–316) is an unsolved mystery. The spectral analysis of a metal ornament showed 10 per cent copper, 5 per cent magnesium and 85 per cent aluminium. Aluminium seemed to be completely out of place in an ancient tomb because it is produced by electrolysis! Tests were repeated, each time with the same results. Does this mean that the Chinese used electricity in the fourth century?

An old manuscript *Agastya Samhita*, preserved in the Indian Princes Library at Ujjain, contains surprising instructions for constructing dry-cell batteries: "A well cleaned copper plate should be placed in an earthenware vessel. It should then be covered first by copper sulphate and then by moist saw-dust. Mercury-amalgamated-zinc plate to prevent polarization should then be placed on the top of the sawdust. By their contact a liquid energy known by the twin name of Mitra-Varuna is produced. Water is split up by this current into Pranavayu and Udanavayu. The joining together of one hundred of such vessels is said to be very active and effective." [49]

"Mitra-Varuna" is easily interpreted as cathode-anode and "Pranavayu" and "Udanavayu" as oxygen and hydrogen. The wise sage Agastya is also known in history as 'Kumbhayoni' from the word 'Kumbha' or jar, in memory of the earthenware jars employed by him in making the batteries. He is also credited with building a 'Pushpaka-vimana' or airship.

Besides the batteries, history has much to say in regard to miracles produced by the ancients. Ovid writes that Numa Pompilius, the second king of Rome, used to invoke Jupiter to light altars by flames from the sky. Numa caused a perpetual light to burn in the dome of a temple which he had built. Pausanias observed a golden lamp in the Temple of Minerva in A.D. 170. It provided illumination for a year without re-fuelling.

Among the tombs near Memphis, the ancient city of Egypt, ever-burning lights have been found in sealed chambers, but after exposure to air the flames went out. Similar perpetual lamps are known to have existed in the Brahmin temples of India.

The statue of Memnon in Egypt spoke as soon as the rays of the rising sun fell upon its mouth. The sound issued from the base of the figure. In the words of Juvenal—"Memnon sounds his magic strings." The Incas had a speaking idol in the valley of Rimac. Needless to say, the construction of these statues required a knowledge of physics.

There are reasons to believe that flashes from the eyes of Egyptian gods, particularly those of Isis, could have been produced by electricity, since strange appliances have been found in Egypt.[38]

Lucian (A.D. 120–80), the Greek satyrist, made a trip to Hierapolis in Northern Syria and described its marvels. He saw a gem on the goddess Hera's head from which flashed a great light—"so that the whole temple gleams brightly as by the light of myriads of candles". There was also another wonder. The eyes of Hera followed a person no matter where he moved. Lucian did not explain the phenomenon because he could not—the priests kept him in the dark about their science.

The colourful frescoes on the walls and ceilings of rock-cut tombs in Egypt must have been painted in bright light. However, daylight never reaches these dark chambers. There are no stains from oil lamps or torches. Was electric light employed in some of them?

The mysteries of the Temple of Hadad or Jupiter at Baalbek were connected with luminous stones. The existence of these stones, providing a source of lighting at night in ancient times, can not be questioned because so many classic writers describe them.

Plutarch wrote in the first century of our era that he had seen a 'perpetual lamp' in the temple of Jupiter Amun and that the priests assured him it had burnt continually for many years. Neither wind nor water could extinguish it. A stone sepulchre of Pallas, the son of Evander, was found in 1401. At the head of the Roman stood a lamp burning with perpetual fire. Nothing could put it out until it was broken to pieces by desecrators. St Augustine (b. A.D. 354) describes an ever-burning lamp he saw at the temple of Venus. Kedrenus (Cedrinus), eleventh-century historian of Byzantium, affirms that he observed a perpetual lamp at Edessa, Syria, where it had burnt for five hundred years.

The Abbe Evariste-Regis Huc (1813–60) claimed that he had examined one of the perpetually burning lamps in Tibet.

Tales of strange lamps come to us from the Americas as well. In 1601 Barco Centenera wrote about the city of Gran Moxo near the source of the Paraguay River in the Matto Grosso. In this account he draws a picture of a mysterious island city from the reminiscences of conquistadores:

> In the middle of the lake was an island on which were buildings of great beauty and splendour, beyond human understanding. The mansion of the Lord, the Gran Moxo, was built of white stone right to the very roof. It had two very high towers at its entrance, and a stairway in the middle. At a pillar in the middle, on the right, were two live lions [jaguars? A.T.] They crouched at its sides, in chains, whose links were of gold. On the summit of this pillar, 25 feet high, was a great moon. It illuminated all the lake, dispelling darkness and shadows by night and day, so that all appeared very bright.

Colonel P. H. Fawcett was told by the natives in the Matto Grosso that mysterious cold lights had been seen by them in the lost cities of the jungle. Writing to Lewis Spence, the British author, he says: "These people have a source of illumination which is strange to us—in fact they are a remnant of civilization which has gone and which has retained old knowledge."

Mandans, the white Indians of North America, remember an age when their ancestors lived in "cities with inextinguishable lights" beyond the ocean. Was it Atlantis? Is it from Atlantean survivors that the ancients inherited these strange lamps?

Only a few decades ago Torres Strait islanders were known to have had 'booya' or round stones which emitted piercing light. These light-belching stones were decorated with shells, hair, teeth and colours. Greenish-blue light, which would flame up from them to a considerable distance, was a complete puzzle to the white men who saw a 'booya'.[50]

A few years ago traders in New Guinea discovered a jungle valley near Mount Wilhelmina populated by amazons. They were terrified to see stone balls about 12 feet in diameter mounted on columns, radiate neon-like light. C. S. Downey, a delegate to the conference on street lighting and traffic in Pretoria, South Africa was so much impressed by the weird but effective form of illumination in this jungle in New Guinea that he stated in 1963: "These women, cut off from the rest of mankind, may have perfected a system of artificial illumination equal, if not superior, to the twentieth century." It is most unlikely that the jungle amazons could have evolved a system of lighting superior to ours. It is more probable that they have inherited the incandescent spheres from a civilization of which there is no record in our histories.

The presence of artificial illumination in antiquity has been attested to by classic writers and folklore. Electra, the shining daughter of Atlas, may be only a symbol for electricity in Atlantis.

ROCKS IN THE AIR

When pre-Inca stonemasonry was uncovered at Ollantaytambo and Sacsahuaman in Peru, the weight of some of the stones was estimated to be over 100 tons. In spite of their great mass, the blocks were put in place with such exactitude that the joints could hardly be seen with the naked eye. No builders anywhere in the world, except Egypt, have ever matched the architects of the megalithic structures of Peru.

The Great or Khufu Pyramid of Egypt is one of the most accurate pieces of construction in the world. Its builders must have had a superior knowledge of geometry and architecture. It has justly been said that Time laughs at everything, but the pyramids laugh at Time.

The 15-ton polished blocks at the base of the Khufu Pyramid are fitted together with an accuracy of one-hundredth of an inch. A thin piece of paper can scarcely be inserted between the blocks. Before our present technological century no nation in history could duplicate such precision.

If we accept the Egyptologists' date for the building of the Great Pyramid, then this structure, which has remained the highest on earth until recent times, was erected in an epoch when there were no cranes or even wheels. Only a century before the commencement of works on the pyramid, the Egyptians were still building in mudbrick. Are we then to believe that in one century the ancient Egyptians made so phenomenal an advance that it took them but twenty years to construct a stone edifice, the tallest until this century?

The question as to how the Khufu Pyramid was built has never been satisfactorily explained. Diodorus Siculus writes that 360,000 men were employed in the erection for twenty years. Herodotus's figures are 100,000 men for twenty years.

According to the Greek historian, this extravagant venture brought Cheops or Khufu to the verge of bankruptcy. The cruel pharaoh then cast out his glamorous daughter from the palace to a trading house which commercialized sex. However, the young woman must have done quite well because "she not only obtained the sum appointed by her father but, on her own account, was minded to leave a memorial behind her, and asked each of her visitors to give her one stone for the works".

It is difficult to accept a story of this type as history. Herodotus could have been purposely misled by the scientist-priests of Egypt who did not want to reveal to him the true purpose of their megalithic structures.

When accurate measurements of the Great Pyramid were made in the nineteenth century, it was disclosed that the angle between each of the sides and the plane of the foundations was 51 degrees 51 seconds to 51 degrees 52 seconds. As the pinnacle of the pyramid was missing, the height of the structure was arrived at by means of geometry. Then in accordance with mathematics, the perimeter of the base was divided by double height with the surprising result of 3·14149 or π.

The mean distance of the earth to the sun is about 149·5 million kilometres. The height of the Cheops Pyramid is 147·8 metres, or the astronomical distance to the sun reduced by a thousand million times, with an error of 1 per cent.

The unit of length used in the construction of the pyramid was the pyramid cubit, equivalent to 635·66 millimetres. The radius of the earth from the centre to pole is 6,357 kilometres —or the pyramid cubit multiplied ten million times.

At the end of the eighteenth century the standard metre was taken to be one forty-millionth of the terrestrial perimeter at Paris. The metre has been found to be incorrect after more precise measurements of the earth in this century. Yet the Egyptian cubit is equal to one ten-millionth of the earth's radius to one-hundredth of a millimetre.

The length of one pyramid side at the base is 365·25 pyramid cubits. But there are also 365·25 days in a year— again a strange coincidence between the proportions of the pyramid and astronomical data. It seems that the blueprints of the Great Pyramid have to be sought in Atlantis.

After a long study of the geometrical dimensions of the Khufu Pyramid, A. K. Abramov, a Moscow engineer, concluded that the pyramid holds an answer to the unsolved problem of mathematics of squaring the circle. He believes that ancient Egyptians had successfully coped with it thanks to the employment of the septenary system in defining π as $22/7$. He has also discovered that they used a 'radian' or $\pi/6$ as a basic unit of measure.

In an interview with the author in Moscow, A. K. Abramov said: "One must, of necessity, consider the historical background which determined the appearance of the quadrature of the circle in actual practice. Let us drift into the depths of the ages for 4,500 years to the time of the construction of the Great Pyramid. Long before its erection rational minds of antiquity cognized many objective facts. The most important among these was the discovery of the relation of the length of the circumference to its diameter—equal to $22/7$ in the septenary system. About the same time discoveries of certain relative truths were also made. To these belong the straightening of the circumference, three sections of an angle, doubling of a cube without modifying its form, conversion of the volumes of cubes into volumes of spheres, etc. It is but natural that the discovered facts were put into objective reality. After all, it has been ascertained that the Khufu Pyramid is so constructed that the perimeter of the base is equal to the circumference, drawn with a radius equal to the pyramid's height.

From the dimensions of the pyramid, expressed in 'radians', this equality of the perimeters of the square and the circle becomes apparent in the following equation where the first shows the length of the four sides of the Khufu Pyramid and the second—that of a circumference drawn with the radius equivalent to the pyramid's height $(2\pi r)$:

$$440 \times 4 = 1760 \qquad 2 \times 22/7 \times 280 = 1760*$$

According to Abramov, ancient Egyptian priests upheld a unique concept of the three dimensions of space. To them a point was the initial point of three directions—of length, breadth and thickness.

"Pythagoras was unable to grasp the richness of the science of geometry which stood before him in Egypt," continued Abramov. "The Egyptian knowledge was superior. It is a great riddle where it came from. That the superior science was there is confirmed by actual facts—the pyramids, which have lasted for ages, speak for the wisdom of their builders.

"The mathematicians may perhaps say: 'Let this unknown science be cursed, let all the pyramids crumble.' After all, it is so much easier to prove that we have reached the apex of civilization and that no one in the past could have had more intelligence than the man of today.

"Lobachevsky demonstrated the universality of space geometry. This great science was somehow brought to the land of Egypt. But by whom and from where? If the original 'Sons of the Sun' were culture-bearers from space then many puzzles are solved. The universal science of geometry proves that life on other planets has probably appeared earlier but followed the same pattern in the field of knowledge as here on earth.

"Another cosmic civilization may have learned how to produce energy by different methods. Perhaps, they could convert light into propulsion energy without any synchrotrons. In that case they may have had spaceships of a different construction than the ones we build today," concluded A. K. Abramov.

When the discussion came to an end, the author recalled a story about Einstein who was once asked: "How are discoveries made?" "When all the scientists present have agreed

* radian = $\pi/6$ = 0·5238095

that something is impossible, one arrives too late for their meeting and solves the impossible," answered Einstein.

The more one studies the pyramids the more one feels that a race of scientific giants built them.

There is a tradition that megalithic monuments were erected by sound vibrations. Gravity was somehow neutralized by incantations, music and magnetized rods which raised stones into the air. This is a fantastic possibility which should be exploited to the full in this age of aviation and astronautics. Arabs have an interesting legend about the building of the Khufu Pyramid: "They put sheets of papyrus on which were written many secret things beneath the stones and then struck them with a rod, whereupon they moved through the air the distance of one bowshot. In this way they eventually reached the pyramid."

The ancients could have mastered the forces of repulsion as much as those of attraction, if their science had a different approach to energy and matter.

The blocks of Baalbek Terrace in Lebanon are fifty to a hundred times heavier than those of the Great Pyramid. Even gigantic cranes of today would be unable to raise them from the foot of the hill to the top on which the platform stands. What Titans built these megalithic edifices in Lebanon, Egypt and Peru?

François Lenormant in his book on Chaldean Magic cites a legend about the priests of On who could by means of sounds raise into the air huge stones which a thousand men could not move. Is this only a myth or folk memory of the feats of a vanished science?

Lucian (A.D. 155) testifies to the reality of 'antigravity' in ancient history when he writes about the effigy of Apollo in a Hierapolis temple. As the priests were raising the god, Apollo "left them on the ground, and was borne aloft himself alone". This occurred in the presence of Lucian himself.

Few people realize that the feats of the ancients in what may be termed 'prehistoric science' take place even today. Near Poona in Western India there is the village of Shivapur on the Satara Road. It has a small memorial mosque dedicated to Qamar Ali Dervish, a Sufi saint. In front of the mosque lie two large round boulders. The bigger granite stone weighs 120 pounds and the smaller 90.

Daily groups of pilgrims and visitors stand around one of the stones, chanting the name of Qamar Ali Dervish in loud ringing tones while their right forefingers touch the boulder. For some reason only eleven people should encircle the larger stone. Suddenly, the rock detaches itself from the ground, becoming completely weightless, and within seconds rises 6 feet in the air, where it remains for a split second before dropping to the ground with a thud. The same thing happens with the other boulder which is levitated by a group of nine.

This peculiar phenomenon occurs many times a day to the indescribable amazement of all who partake in the manifestation, or watch it. Normally, it takes six men to lift the larger granite boulder by a strong grip. There must be a solid scientific explanation of this levitation because anyone can take part in the stone-raising—Mohammedan, Brahmin, Buddhist, Christian or agnostic. The different people who daily perform the feat, can never tell how it is accomplished.

Despite all scepticism, the fact remains that a heavy stone rises 6 feet in the air against all laws of physics. In this Space Age, when top scientists are trying to solve the secret of gravity, this strange phenomenon deserves a serious investigation. Whether the sound waves from the rhythmic incantation, bio-currents from the forefingers, or their joint effects produce degravitation of the boulders—is a matter for speculation. However, if the words "Qamar Ali Dervish" are not pronounced in loud, clear tones, the stones do not rise.

This wonder of India can serve today as a possible demonstration of the method by which the pyramids and other megaliths might have been erected in antiquity.

RELICS CREATE A DILEMMA

Muhiddin Piri Reis, or Admiral Piri Reis (1470–1554), published in Turkey a navigation atlas *Bahriyye* in 1520. His maps with marginal notes, drawn on roe-skin, were discovered at the palace of Topkapi in Istanbul on 9 November 1929 by Halil Edhem, Director of the National Museums.

In his notes Admiral Piri reveals the story of his maps. In a naval battle with Spain in 1501, a Turkish officer Kemal took prisoner a Spaniard who had been with Columbus on three of his historic voyages. The captive had a set of curious maps.

Christopher Columbus may have known where he was going thanks to these maps. If this supposition is correct then we can understand the words of his son Ferdinand who wrote in *The Life of the Admiral Christopher Columbus* that: "He noted down any helpful hints that sailors or other persons might drop. He made such good use of all these things that he grew convinced beyond the shadow of a doubt, that to the west of the Canary and Cape Verde Islands lay many lands which could be reached and discovered."

Among the articles confiscated by the Turks from the Spaniard were the maps drawn by Columbus in 1498, or six years after the discovery of the West Indies. Yet the charts show a complete outline of the continents of North and South America, their rivers, Greenland and Antarctica—all unknown in 1498. The distance between South America and Africa is surprisingly correct.

Professor Dr Afetinan of Turkey in his book *The Oldest Map of America* writes: "In the chapter on this 'Western Sea' we read all that is known about the discovery of America at the time. Of this he (Piri Reis, A. T.) recounts, on hearsay again, how a certain book from the time of Alexander the Great was translated in Europe and after reading it how Christopher Columbus went and discovered the Antilles with the vessels he obtained from the Spanish government. It is quite evident today that Piri Reis came into possession of the map that the great discoverer used." [51]

Many things are puzzling about the Piri Reis map. Who drew a chart in Columbus's or perhaps even in Alexander the Great's times with the contours of Antarctica free of ice, and how did he do it? After all, it is only in the International Geophysical Year that the continent was sounded through the ice sheet and charted. Greenland is shown as two or three islands. Greenland is buried under 5,000 feet of glaciers and it is only recently that a French Polar expedition disclosed the fact that Greenland comprises two main islands.

Arlington H. Mallery, an American authority on cartography,

asked the U.S. Hydrographic Office to check the enigmatic map. Commander Larsen, on behalf of U.S. Navy, then made a statement: "The Hydrographic Office of the Navy has verified an ancient chart—it's called the Piri Reis map, that goes back more than 5,000 years. It's so accurate, only one thing could explain it—a world-wide survey. The Hydrographic Office couldn't believe it, either, at first. But they not only proved the map genuine, it's been used to correct errors in some present-day maps."

According to Mallery, the archaic chart had a record of every mountain range in Northern Canada and Alaska, including some ranges which the U.S. Army Map Services did not have on their maps. But the U.S. Army has since found them.

The longitude on this map is exact. This is baffling as it is only two hundred years since we learned how to calculate it. Mallery even remarked: "We do not know how they could map so accurately without an aeroplane."

This map demonstrates the existence of science in a faraway epoch which is considered to have possessed none. Did the expedition of Alexander the Great come into possession of papyri from the temple of Sais in Egypt? Its priests definitely knew about America for, as Plato writes, Solon was told that the Atlantic "is a real sea and the surrounding land may be most truly called a continent."

The arguments set forth in favour of the very ancient origin of the Piri Reis map which Christopher Columbus allegedly possessed, can be substantiated by another startling fact. Space satellites have disclosed that our planet is somewhat pear-shaped. A letter from Columbus is still extant in which he states that the earth is 'pear-shaped'. Two decades ago we did not know about the strange form of our planet. How did Columbus learn about it?

The Azerbaijan mathematician and astronomer of the thirteenth century, Nasireddin Tusi, was also somehow aware of the existence of America, 220 years before Columbus. G. D. Mamedbeily of the Azerbaijan Academy of Sciences has recently found out that seven centuries ago the scholar mentioned in his works the land of "Dzhezair Haldat" (eternal isles), the geographical co-ordinates of which correspond exactly to the eastern contour of South America. Like the enigmatical Piri Reis map, Nasireddin Tusi's manuscript must have had archaic science for its source.

The Arab astronomer Abul Wafa (A.D. 939–98) discovered irregularity in the moon's motion, known as the variation. This deviation of the moon from the regular path is caused by differences in the sun's pull at various points of the lunar orbit. It is impossible to observe this without a good clock and precision instruments which the Baghdad astronomer did not have in the tenth century.

It was about seven hundred years later that Tycho de Brahe announced his discovery of the variation of the moon, and he is credited with it in astronomy. However, some astronomers have referred to the treatise of the Arab savant who seemed to have known about it long before Tycho de Brahe. Others have claimed it was impossible for Abul Wafa to have made this discovery.

How is it possible that the sages of old knew more about certain things than they were supposed to? The mystery could be explained once the existence of traditional knowledge is admitted. From Egypt, India, Greece and other countries this secret science of the ages was imported into Europe veiled in alchemical, astrological and Rosicrucian symbology to avoid the persecution of the all-powerful Inquisition.

It is not inconceivable that some secret fraternities have preserved books from the Alexandrian Library. Perhaps premature discovery of the variation of the moon by Abul Wafa may become clear in this light.

Jonathan Swift in his *Gulliver's Travels* described the two moons of Mars in 1726. He called them "lesser stars, or satellites". Swift wrote that the innermost one orbits Mars in ten hours and the outermost in twenty-one and a half hours.

The American astronomer Asaph Hall discovered the two satellites of Mars in 1877, or about 150 years after Jonathan Swift's book. The two Martian moons have since been named Phobos and Deimos. Phobos, the inner moonlet, rotates around its mother planet in 7 hours 39 minutes and Deimos, the outer satellite, in 30 hours 18 minutes. Though Swift's figures do not coincide with the actual periods of rotation of the two small moons of Mars, they are not very far from them.

We read in *Gulliver's Travels* that the innermost satellite, now called Phobos, orbits Mars at the distance of three of the planet's diameters, or 12,600 miles. According to Swift, the outer moon or Deimos revolves around the planet at the distance of five Martian diameters from its centre, or 21,000 miles. The author of *Gulliver's Travels* somewhat erred in his figures, as the actual distances of the moons from the centre of Mars are 5,826 miles for Phobos and 14,580 for Deimos. Irrespective of these inaccuracies, the similarity between the hypothetical satellites of Jonathan Swift and the real ones is too close to be coincidental. Did Swift have access to some rare manuscripts of great age?

The so-called Voynich manuscript, estimated to be about four hundred and fifty years old, is considered to be the most mysterious document in the world. It was on sale in New York for $160,000 in 1962.[52]

The relic was found by Wilford W. Voynich, a New York antiquary, in a castle near Rome in 1912. The handwriting, style of drawings, type of vellum and ink indicate that the manuscript was written about A.D. 1500.

It is written in cipher and contains illustrations of plants, symbols and figures rendered in the style of ancient alchemical and hermetic diagrams. Originally it had 272 pages but twenty-six are missing. On the last sheet there is an inscription in Latin: "Thou wert opening to me many gates."

In the puzzling charts are found drawings which appear to be cross-sections of leaves and roots. Sixteen have been identified as actual European species. But the sketches could not have been made without a microscope, supposedly non-existent in 1500. Also this antique book has a picture of what may be taken for the Andromeda Galaxy, visible as a spiral only through a telescope.

Wartime code experts in Washington, who had cracked the complex ciphers of Japan and Germany, failed to decipher the Voynich manuscript. This scientific riddle can be put in the same class as the Piri Reis map. Abul Wafa's discovery of lunar variation, Jonathan Swift's Martian satellites. They may all come from the treasury of prehistoric science.

The concept of a master culture from which our postdiluvian civilization derives its source, is within the bounds of scientific reasoning.

Professor Frederick Soddy, one of the founders of nuclear physics, speaking about traditions of antiquity asks if they "may not point to the existence of an ancient, totally unknown and unsuspected civilization of which all other traces have disappeared".[17]

Our science is not a fountain gushing fresh from the barren rock. It is rather like a long stream fed by far-off rivulets. The greater part of our knowledge comes from a forgotten past.

SKYSHIPS OF ANTIQUITY

It is quite reasonable to surmise that most of the legends about skyships in olden times are echoes of aviation and astronautics from a former civilization. Despite the strong opposition to the theory of an advanced technology in the dim past, coming from the majority of scientists, there are numerous facts which support this hypothesis.

The *Ramayana* of India contains detailed descriptions of a "vimana" or airship. It was self-propelled by a yellowish-white liquid. The vimana was large—it had two stories, windows, dome with a pinnacle. The airship of antiquity could fly with the "speed of the wind" according to one's skill, and gave forth a "melodious sound". Its control required high intelligence. The craft could travel in the sky or stop and remain motionless in the air.

The vimanas were kept in "vimana griha" or hangars. The ancient records state that the vimana soared above the clouds and from the altitude "the ocean looked like a small pool of water". The aviator could see the "country round about the ocean and the mouths of rivers meeting the ocean".[49]

The archaic planes were employed in warfare by kings and for sport by the "foremost people among pleasure seekers". It is most unlikely that such precise details could be mere fancy.

In China the Emperor Shun, who lived about 4,200 years

ago, constructed a flying chariot. Shun is not only the first recorded pilot but also the first parachutist.[44]

Chu Yuan (340–278 B.C.) wrote a description of an air trip in a poem called "Li Sao". As he knelt at the grave of the Emperor Shun, a jade chariot drawn by four dragons appeared. Chu Yuan boarded the craft and flew at a high altitude across China in the direction of the Kun Lun Range. In his aerial journey he observed the earth, unaffected by the winds and dust of the Gobi. Chu Yuan not only successfully landed upon the completion of the flight but also subsequently made another survey of the Kun Lun Mountains from the air.[53]

The founder of the Shang dynasty, the Emperor Cheng Tang (1766 B.C.) ordered Ki Kung Shi to build a flying chariot. The ancient engineer completed the assignment and tested the aircraft in flight, reaching the province of Honan. However, the vessel was destroyed by imperial edict so that the secret of its mechanism would not fall into wrong hands.[44]

The flying machines of ancient China were either a product of scientific experimentation or a memory from a precataclysmic race. As the Chinese had no technology at the time, there is no alternative but to accept the second possibility.

Chu Yuan's flight to the Kun Lun may, perhaps, give us the clue to the source of this technical knowledge in ancient China. The mighty Kun Lun Range is considered by the Chinese people to be the abode of 'gods'.

These skyships were traditionally reserved for the Emperors and Taoist scholars who were supposed to act as intermediaries between the 'genii of the mountains' and mankind.

An indirect proof of our theory that in ancient times man knew of aviation, is found in the presence of the words 'flying chariot' in Chinese vocabulary. When confronted with the appearance of the aeroplane early in this century, the Chinese did not have, like ourselves, to invent a new term—they used the old one—fei chi (flying chariot).

In the twelfth year of the Emperor Yao's reign (2346 B.C.) a strange man appeared. His name was Chih Chiang Tzu-yu. He was so skilful an archer that the Emperor named him 'Divine Archer' and appointed him 'Chief Mechanician'.

In the annals of Chinese history he is reported to have ridden a 'celestial bird'. When "carried into the centre of an immense horizon" he noticed that he could no longer observe the rotary movement of the sun. In space, beyond the earth, our astronauts are also unable to see the sun rise or set. Does the ancient record of the 'Chief Mechanician's' flight intimate that man could bridge interplanetary space thousands of years ago?

The great Chinese thinker Chuang Tzu wrote an essay entitled "Travel to the Infinite" in the third century before our era. He relates how he rode on the back of a fabulous bird of enormous size into space to the distance of 32,500 miles from the earth.[54]

According to Taoist beliefs 'Chen Jen' or perfect men, are able to fly through the air on the wings of the wind. They pass on the clouds from one world to another and live in the stars.[55] Teng Mu, a scholar of the Sung dynasty, wrote about "other skies and other earths". Ma Tse Jan, a distinguished physician of old China, after having mastered the philosophy of Taoism, was taken to heaven alive.

In his travels through Tibet and Mongolia Professor Nicholas Roerich saw passages in Buddhist books about "iron serpents which devour space with fire and smoke" and "inhabitants of the distant stars".[20]

Viaches! v Zaitsev in the Soviet magazine *Neman* (No. 12, 1966) wri s about strange stone discs discovered in the district of Baian-Kara-Ula on the border of China and Tibet. They have holes in the centres like gramophone records. A double groove inscribed with hieroglyphics spirals from the centre to the edge of the discs.

Professor Tsum-Um-Nui, with four colleagues, has deciphered the writing in the grooves. However, their discovery was so sensational that at first the Peking Academy of Prehistory did not allow the Chinese scientists to publish their findings. After the permission had been granted, a book appeared under an intriguing title, *Disc Hierolglyphics speak of Spaceships 12,000 years ago*.

An analysis of the stone particles from the discs revealed amazing results—they contained a large quantity of cobalt and some other metal. Tested under an oscillograph the discs displayed a peculiar frequency as if they had been electrically charged thousands of years ago.

The carvings of Baian-Kara-Ula discs depict the sun, moon and the stars as well as some strange dots gliding from the sky towards the earth.

Tschi Pen Lao, of the University of Peking, has discovered curious drawings in the mountains of Hunan and on an island in Lake Tungting. Made about 45,000 B.C. these granite carvings portray people with large trunks and cylindrical craft. It is difficult to admit the existence of spacehelmets and spaceships so long ago—yet what other explanation can one offer?

From the study of myths and historical records it follows that men flying heavenward and cosmic guests coming earthward were a reality in a bygone age. Whether these space visitors came from another planet or from a secret Atlantean colony in a remote part of our globe, is largely a matter for speculation. However, there is no contradiction between the two versions if we assume, on the basis of available data, that Atlantis had contacts with other planetary civilizations.

In an article, "By the Path of Legends", U. Tkachev, writing in the Soviet magazine *Smena*, stresses the usefulness of imagination in the field of science. Because of the affinity of his ideas with the plot of the present book we will cite it:

The earth was visited by an expedition of cosmonauts. It is upon the continent of Atlantis that the spaceship landed. Apparently the earth was not their principal base as otherwise their stay would have left more definite traces. Evidently the astronauts possessed such a technology that they could construct satellites with their own peculiar conditions for life. Using these as bases, they reached the earth and other planets in 'planetoplanes'. Presumably they acquainted the Atlanteans with but few branches of culture, none of which could be employed for enslaving the neighbouring peoples because of their immeasurable humaneness. In all likelihood, these were—painting, sculpture, architecture, mathematics and astronomy. Possibly they had visited the earth a number of times and these flights were recorded in folklore as the descents of gods upon the earth. The Atlanteans founded the first state in the history of earth. Their continent sank 11,500 years ago. The principal site of culture perished. Knowledge was gradually lost by mankind. Occasionally ancient science would come to the surface.[56]

Dr Carl Sagan, an American astrophysicist of the first magnitude, has made interesting conclusions on the basis of mathematical computations. He suggests that if each advanced civilization in our galaxy sends a spaceship once a year by our time reckoning, in the direction of neighbouring stars, the interval between cosmic vists would be equal to about 5,500 years. According to Dr Sagan's calculations, the explorers from other solar systems are soon to fly over us on their regular inspection tour. Upon landing on earth the cosmonauts would be greatly surprised at the progress mankind has achieved since the first dynasty in ancient Egypt.

Incidentally, the tradition of Aztecs speaks of a promise of the 'sons of heaven' to return in 6,000 years—that is in our historical epoch.[57]

Dr C. Sagan believes that "the earth may have been visited many times by various galactic civilizations during geological times and it is not out of the question that artifacts of these visits still exist".[58] The American scientist recommends us not to discard ancient myths which may contain accounts of appearances of space visitors described as 'gods' or 'angels' in scriptures and folklore.

Today the reaction of simple men and women who have never seen an automobile or aeroplane in some isolated part of the world, would be much the same as the one shown by the ancients when confronted with the appearance of a strange apparatus. In the fifties a jeep was dismantled, carried over the 13,400-foot Rohtang Pass in the Himalayas, and reassembled on the Lahoul side. As it descended into a valley, the surprised natives who had never seen a mechanically propelled vehicle, came out to worship this manifestation of supernatural power. When the first plane landed in Ladakh in 1948, the reaction of Tibetans to this flying monster was even more comic—they brought hay to feed it.

K. E. Tsiolkovsky, the Russian pioneer in astronautics, when asked to express his opinion on the probability of inter-planetary contacts, said that the visitation of our planet by cosmonauts could have taken place in the past, and would indeed occur in the future.[59]

Faced with the same question in 1930 Professor N. A. Rynin of U.S.S.R. answered that "if we turn to tales and legends of hoary antiquity, we will notice strange coincidences among legends of countries separated by oceans and deserts. These coincidences in legends comprise the visitation of earth by dwellers of other worlds in time immemorial. Why not admit that a grain of truth still lies in the kernels of these legends?" [59]

If beings from other planets paid us visits in a forgotten epoch, then it is clear how fruits and grains unknown to earth were brought by the 'gods' from other 'lokas' or worlds, as Brahmin books claim.

The subject of cosmic contacts in past ages, possibly in the Atlantean era, has been contemplated by men of science. It is assuredly worthy of a serious consideration in this Space Age, when we ourselves are about to explore other planets.

Behind legends can be dimly discerned a distant epoch in which a vanished race might have attained to a high degree of technology.

CHAPTER SEVEN

PRE-DELUGE TREASURE VAULTS

ARCHAIC MUSEUMS

Let us recollect the words of the Egyptian priest Sonchis of Sais who said this to Solon, the Greek lawgiver: "You are all young in your souls; for you have not any old tradition, any ancient belief nor knowledge that is hoary with age. And the reason of it is this: many have been the destructions of mankind, and many shall be."

It appears from this phrase that the Egyptians had records going back for thousands of years. Otherwise it would have been impossible for the priest to convey to Solon the story of Atlantis in an exact manner.

Atlantis may be viewed as just another myth. If the ancient Greek legend of Troy turned out to be history after Schliemann, should not more credence be given to folklore as well as to the writings of historians in the classic world?

Cicero (106–43 B.C.) writes in *De Divinatione* that the Babylonian priests "assert that they have preserved upon monuments observations extending back during an interval of 470,000 years". We thank the haughty Roman for recording this fact and forgive him his jeers.

Over 2,000 years ago Strabo mentioned the Iberians of Spain who "are acquainted with writing and have works devoted to the history of their race, poems and laws expressed in verse— 6,000 years old as they claim".

Diogenes Laertius wrote in the third century of our era that the ancient Egyptians had recorded 373 solar and 832 lunar eclipses. On the basis of the periodicity of eclipses it can be estimated that these observations covered approximately 10,000 years.

The 4,000-year-old *Epic of Gilgamesh* says that Gilgamesh "was wise, he saw mysteries and knew secret things, he brought us a tale of the days before the Flood. He went on a long journey, was weary, worn-out with labour, and returning engraved on a stone the whole story".

The pyramids of Babylon, or ziggurats, were tiered towers with a religious and astronomical meaning. Were they constructed over or near hidden vaults sheltering the records of mankind for vast periods of time, as Babylonian priests claimed?

Let us leave the Babylonians and travel to Egypt. Before us is Manetho, a priest and keeper of the sacred archives of the temple of Heliopolis. The date is third century before our era. Manetho is known to have extracted his story of the past from pillars in secret subterranean temples of Egypt near Thebes, not far from the sounding statue of Memnon. Eusebius (A.D. 265–340) remarks in his writings that Manetho studied history from inscriptions on columns made by Thoth (Hermes). After the deluge these records were translated and transcribed on scrolls by Agatodaemon, the second son of Hermes, and then deposited in unknown temple vaults.

Historical tradition of the ancients affirms that these enormous underground repositories were constructed on orders of the sages of Atlantis who had anticipated the coming of a world cataclysm. The Byzantine historian George the Syncellus (d. A.D. 806) wrote of the chronicles which the ancient Egyptians had kept for 36,525 years.

Proclus (A.D. 412–489) writes that Plato visited Egypt and conversed at Sais with the highpriest Pateneit, at Heliopolis with the priest Ochlapi and at Sebennytus with the hierophant Ethimon. It is possible that during his Egyptian tour Plato was given first-hand information on Atlantis.

Crantor (300 B.C.) says that in Egypt there were certain pillars in secret places which contained the history of Atlantis in hieroglyphics, and these were shown to some Greeks.

In writing about the pyramids Ammianus Marcellinus (A.D. 330–400), a Roman historian, adds his testimony to the reality of the vaults with chronicles concealed in Egypt: "There are also subterranean passages and winding retreats, which, it is said, men skilful in the ancient mysteries, by means of which they divined the coming of a flood, constructed in different places lest the memory of all their sacred ceremonies should be lost."

The writings of the ancients are silent as to the exact location of these retreats. Manetho learned history in one of these hidden halls of records. Solon, from whom Plato indirectly obtained the legend of Atlantis, must also have been given access to a secret depository by his Egyptian hosts.

About 2,500 years ago Herodotus was shown 345 statues of Egyptian high priests in lineal succession up to 11,340 years before his time. Herodotus also writes that Osiris appeared 15,000 years before Amasis, who reigned between 570 and 526 B.C., and adds—"they claim to be quite certain of these dates, for they have always kept a careful written record of the passage of time".

Is the Khufu Pyramid a monument to mark the location of a secret treasury of Atlantean culture built before the Flood? This question may seem to be ludicrous yet Manetho maintained that the pyramid had not been erected by Egyptians. When Herodotus visited Egypt in 455 B.C. he definitely established that the megalithic structure contained nothing resembling burial remains.

The theory of secret chambers in or under the pyramids and the Sphinx should not remain in the realm of speculation. It is when theory is converted into practice that discoveries are made.

Where to look for the ancient vaults and how to reach them? If the storehouses are not within the pyramids, their position and depth underground may be ascertained by finding some sort of a geometrical pattern in the layout of the Sphinx and the pyramids. The message could be hidden in mathematical proportions of the structures. On the other hand, there may be an astronomical key to the riddle.

All data about hidden vaults in classic, Egyptian and Arab sources must be carefully analyzed for any possible clues as to the site. Scientific equipment should be employed in solving the riddle of the ages.

The United Arab Republic-United States of America 'Pyramid Project' conducted by the Ein Shams University of Cairo and the University of California—is a step in the right direction.

The scientists have used sensitive electronic 'spark chambers' to measure the flow of cosmic rays from outer space passing through the pyramids. Since cosmic rays strike the pyramids uniformly from all directions, a hollow in the mass of stone above the 'spark chambers' would let more rays through than would the solid parts of pyramids. This would show as shadows on the readings and by using two counters in different positions the exact location of a vault could be pinpointed.

If the 'time capsules' of Atlantis are buried deep under the pyramids, their detection would require a different technique. Ancient tradition speaks of moving walls, secret doors and flashes of light in the depths of the pyramid passages. A generator with an unlimited supply of power could produce these phenomena. Geiger counters or apparati sensitive to the disturbance of a magnetic field may detect its presence. As I wrote to Dr L. W. Alvarez of the University of California, the originator of the Pyramid Project, an extended probe of this type could assume the significance of the first atom bomb or Sputnik I, if the prehistoric vaults are actually discovered.

The Atlantean depository may contain exhibits of predeluge science and technology. Archaic machines may reveal to us new principles of engineering. A gift from the remote past may change our path to the future.

These reflections may seem to be on the brink of fantasy. Yet let us review the developments of the Pyramid X-ray Probe originated early in 1967.

It would be appropriate to mention here that in August 1966 the author wrote to Dr Luis Alvarez, the founder of the Pyramid Project, and suggested that the search for vaults be extended to the foundations of the pyramid by the employment of equipment other than the cosmic-ray counters, in order to sound the ground under the pyramids.

In April 1967 my article "The Pyramid Project" appeared in the Moscow *Komsomoletz*. It said that:

this scientific exploration has been called a 'happy marriage of ancient Egyptology and modern physics'.
What can archaeologists and historians expect from

the sounding of the Giza pyramids? Quite possibly—nothing, if the X-raying will not give the desired results. However, if secret storehouses or tombs are discovered by this method, the scientists will probably be more excited about this event than they were at the time of the opening of Tutankhamen's tomb. Perhaps new chapters will be added to the history of ancient Egypt which have so many torn pages.

In a Sunday issue of the same Soviet newspaper on 26 November 1967 another article of mine was published:

About a thousand years ago the Arabs wrote of moving walls in the pyramid galleries and of secret doors moved by an unknown force. There are accounts concerning robots guarding the treasures and about flashes of brilliant light in the depths of the pyramids. If these are not tales from "One Thousand and One Nights", and if the Arab chroniclers recorded accurately and truthfully, then their stories lead to the supposition that there may be a large power generator under the pyramids or the Sphinx, which was the source of power producing these miraculous phenomena.

Geiger counters and detectors of magnetic field disturbances are not costly but they can bring about unexpected discoveries in archaeology.

In 1969 the Cosmic-Ray exploration at Giza took an unforeseen turn. It was aptly described by John Tunstall in the *Times* Saturday Review for 26 July 1969:

Scientists who have been trying to X-ray the Pyramid of Khephren at Giza, near Cairo, are baffled by mysterious influences which are throwing into utter confusion the readings of their Space Age electronic equipment.

The equipment was demonstrated with dramatic success at the New York World's Fair and the agreement for the joint U.A.R.-United States pyramid project was signed on 14 June 1966. Between 1966 and early 1967 the cosmic ray measuring equipment was installed in the burial chamber at the base line of Khephren's pyramid.

On his second visit to Giza John Tunstall interviewed Dr Amr Gohed, the Arab scientist in charge of the installation at the Khephren pyramid. This is his story:

He showed me the new I.B.M. 1130 machine surrounded by hundreds of tins of recordings from the pyramid stacked in date order. Though hesitant at first, he eventually told me of the complete impasse that had been reached.

"It defies all the known laws of science and electronics," he said, picking up a tin of recordings made in October, 1968. He put the tape through the computer, which traced the pattern of cosmic ray particles on paper. He then selected a recording of the next day in October and put it through the computer. But the recorded pattern was completely different. The salient points which should be repeated on each tape were absent.

"This is scientifically impossible," he told me. But it is happening before the scientists' eyes.

After long discussion and many cups of Arabian coffee, I put the ultimate question to Dr Gohed: "Has all this scientific know-how been rendered useless by some force beyond man's comprehension?" He hesitated before replying, then said: "Either the geometry of the pyramid is in substantial error, which would affect our readings, or there is a mystery which is beyond explanation—call it what you will, occultism, the curse of the Pharaohs, sorcery, or magic, there is some force that defies the laws of science at work in the pyramids."

This is a tremendously significant development at Giza. Where does this force field come from? What superior science and technology created it? As modern physics cannot neutralize cosmic rays, the prehistoric engineers must have had a superior science.

And so the Treasure of the Sphinx still awaits discovery.

The claims of Egyptian and Babylonian priests that their chronicles were hundreds of centuries old, appear to be gross exaggerations. However, it is known that the Serapeum and Brucheum in Alexandria contained well over half a million priceless manuscripts. The discovery of only a portion of these documents today could change our views on ancient history overnight.

The Alexandrian Library has aptly been called the birth-place of modern science. The progress of humanity could have been accelerated if European civilization had received all of its heritage.

It was Cleopatra who closed the list of ancient Egyptian monarchs. As the last ruler of the land of the pharaohs she may have ordered the burial of archives and papyri in sub-terranean vaults.

There is a tradition that shortly before the burning of Alexandria by the Romans, some sacred books of Egypt from its libraries were concealed in a secret place. It is said that the location of the vault containing these precious scrolls is allegedly known to a few initiates of an ancient fraternity.[60]

Julius Caesar set fire to the Egyptian fleet in Alexandria, and this fire spread to the city and destroyed the Brucheum. Diocletian restored the libraries but Aurelian had the Brucheum razed to the ground again. Christian fanatics pillaged the Serapeum in the reign of Theodosius. History does not tell us what happened to the stolen books. Perhaps, a number of scrolls got into the worthy hands of those who, thinking about future generations, buried them in a safe place.

H. P. Blavatsky intimated in her work *Isis Unveiled* that in a Greek monastery is preserved a rare manuscript of Theodas, a scribe of the famous Alexandrian Library. She claimed to have seen a copy of this document in the hands of a monk. It alleges that shortly before Julius Caesar entered Egypt, the library was undergoing repairs. Previous to this, the most precious parchment rolls had been removed to the house of one of the librarians.

When the fire started by the Romans consumed Cleopatra's treasure-house of books, it was generally taken for granted that the withdrawn papyri were also burned. However, they had been rescued by the effort of librarians who might have anticipated fires in wartime.

Blavatsky's communicator, who had a copy of Theodas' document, told her that when the right time came, many more would see this ancient report on the fate of the great library. It would reveal where to look for historical scrolls safely hidden away. The monk stated that thousands of the choicest books were stored in Asia. Truth or fable?

ARABIAN TALES

Masoudi (tenth century), repeating traditions of the Copts (the descendants of ancient Egyptians), says in Manuscript No. 9576 in British Museum that the pyramids "were inscribed with the unknown and unintelligible writings of people and of nations whose names and existence have been long since forgotten". It must be pointed out here that the casings of the pyramids were used up by Arabs as free building material in comparatively recent times.

Herodotus saw the inscriptions on the sides of the pyramids in the fifth century before our era. Ibn Haukal, an Arab traveller and writer of the tenth century, states that the writing on the pyramid casings was still visible in his time. Abd el Latif (twelfth century) writes that the inscriptions on the exterior of the pyramids could fill ten thousand pages.

Ibn Batuta (fourteenth century) another Arab scholar, writes that: "The pyramids were constructed by Hermes to preserve the arts and sciences and other scientific acquirements during the Flood." The Dictionary of Firazabadi (fourteenth century) states that the pyramids were supposed to "preserve the arts and sciences and other knowledge during the deluge". The Coptic papyrus from the monastery of Abou Hormeis has the following passage: "In this manner were the pyramids built. Upon the walls were written the mysteries of science, astronomy, geometry, physic, and much useful knowledge, which any person who understands our writing can read."

Masoudi recorded strange tales about the pyramids. He writes that Surid, a king of Egypt three hundred years before the Flood, built two great pyramids for his 'time capsules'. The priests told him about a great flood and afterwards a fire that would come from 'the constellation of Leo'. Then the pharaoh ordered the pyramids to be erected as a storehouse for all kinds of wonders and treasures. On the walls and ceilings of the pyramid were engraved such sciences as astronomy, mathematics and medicine. Masoudi describes automata or robots which were placed to guard the treasures and destroy "all persons except those who by their conduct were worthy of admission".

Ibn Abd Hokm, ninth-century Arab historian, left a rare account of the building of the pyramids, an extract from which is cited below:

> The greatest part of chronologers agree that he who built the pyramids was Saurid Ibn Salhouk, king of Egypt, who lived three hundred years before the Flood. The occasion of this was because he saw in his sleep that the whole earth was turned over, with the inhabitants of it, the men lying upon their faces, and the stars falling down and striking one another with a terrible noise; and being troubled, he concealed it. Awakening with great fear, he assembled the chief priests of all the provinces of Egypt, one hundred and thirty in number, the chief of whom was Aclimon, and related the whole matter to them. They took the altitude of the stars and making their prognostications, foretold of a deluge. The king said: "Will it come to our country?" They answered: "Yes, and will destroy it." But there remained a certain number of years for it to come, and he commanded in the meantime to build the pyramids with vaults. He filled them with talismans, strange things, riches, treasures and the like. Then he built in the western pyramid thirty treasuries, filled with store of riches and utensils, cartouches made of precious stones, instruments of iron, vessels of clay, arms which did not rust, and glass which could be bent and yet not broken.

The lines about "arms which did not rust" and "glass which

could be bent and yet not broken" are very significant. In the tenth century no one could have imagined such materials as non-corrosive iron or plastics. Undoubtedly, this Arab manuscript has its source in much more ancient writings.

In the British Museum manuscripts Add. 5927 and 7319 from the pen of Ben Yahya Altelemsani, it is mentioned that a subterranean passage from the Great Pyramid reaches the Nile. Also it contains an intriguing account about an article found by Arabs in the pyramid in the ninth century:

> In the days of Ahmed Ben Touloun a party entered the Great Pyramid. They found in one of the chambers a goblet or glass of rare colour and texture. When they came back they missed one of the party and upon returning to seek him, he came out to them naked, and laughing said, "do not follow or seek for me", and then rushed back into the pyramid. They perceived that he was enchanted, and told the circumstances to Ahmed Ben Touloun, who forbade that any should enter the pyramid, and took possession of the goblet of glass, which was afterwards weighed, and found to be of the same weight when empty, and when full of water.

Another Arab writer by the name of Muterdi relates the following story about the exploration of the well of the Khufu Pyramid. A party came to a narrow passage in which were numbers of large bats and down which a current of air was felt. All of a sudden, the walls closed in and cut off a man from the rest of the party. In fright all ran for their lives. Later on the missing member of the group re-appeared and spoke to them in an unknown language. Other versions say that the man dropped dead.

It is easy to dispose of these Arab tales as stories out of *One Thousand and One Nights*. If true, they point to "time capsules" left by a technologically advanced race. The scientific value of their discovery should not be underestimated.

THE RIDDLE OF THE SPHINX SOLVED
The riddle of the Theban Sphinx—"What is that which is four-

113

footed, two-footed and three-footed?"—was correctly guessed by Oedipus who said it was man as a child, adult and old man with a stick.

But the riddle of the Sphinx of Gizeh, resting by the pyramids like a watchdog, has remained unsolved since the times of the pharaohs.

If I may be permitted a personal reminiscence—I have stood before the Sphinx and meditated upon the age and purpose of this wonder of antiquity.

The peculiar type of uraeus on the head of the Sphinx links it with Egypt's earliest sculptures. The granite slab between its legs records that once the young prince Thutmose was hunting near Gizeh and, being tired, lay down by the Sphinx. In a dream the Sphinx began to speak and asked the prince to remove the engulfing sand which covered his body. The reward for this service was to be the throne of Egypt. Thutmose agreed and had the sand removed and a wall built around the Sphinx to protect it from the dunes. Shortly he became Pharaoh Thutmose IV (1682–73 B.C.).

The important point about this story is that the Sphinx was buried to its neck in sand thirty-seven centuries ago. This speaks for the very ancient origin of the Lion-Man even in that distant epoch.

The ancient Egyptians called the monument 'Hu' or protector. From early times tradition held that a secret chamber existed under the Sphinx. Does 'Hu' guard a pre-deluge vault with records?

It is a challenge to solve the riddle of the Sphinx of the Nile and read its message to mankind.

Besides the name of 'Protector' the Sphinx was also called 'Horem-akhet' or 'Horus-in-the-Horizon'. Horus was a falcon sky-god. This name suggests an astronomical solution of the problem. It may refer to the position of the sun on the horizon, or in the zodiac. If for a working hypothesis at least, it is assumed that the Sphinx has an astronomical meaning, then the ancient puzzle can be reduced to clear-cut terms.

First, let us take into account that according to tradition the Flood devastated the world when the sun rose in Leo at vernal equinox.

114

The Zodiac of Denderah, oddly opening with the sign of Leo or Lion, registers the entry into a new cycle between 10,950 and 8,800 B.C.

A Coptic papyrus *Abou Hormeis* (translated into Arabic in ninth century) indicates the date of the Atlantean cataclysm: "The deluge was to take place when the heart of the Lion entered into the first minute of the head Cancer." From the scholar Makrizi (fifteenth century) we learn that "fire was to proceed from the sign Leo, and to consume the world". These ancient sources imply that the zodiacal sign of Leo or Lion was the time, in the precession of equinoxes, when Atlantis came to an end and a new cycle was born. From the Book of the Dead we learn that the movement of the sun in the sky was guarded by two lion gods or 'Akeru' which stood at the morning and evening gates.

Because of its lion-like body, the Sphinx is a guardian god and its significance should be sought in the solar cycle—the Great Year or the precession of equinoxes.

The body of the Sphinx is that of a lion, which symbolises the cycle of Leo. Its head is that of a man. In the zodiac there is only one male figure and that is in the sign of Aquarius. It is exactly on the opposite side of the zodiac from Leo. The message of the Sphinx reads: "From the epoch of Leo to the future age of Aquarius." What does the Sphinx offer to the Aquarian cycle which is soon opening? A 'time capsule' hidden somewhere under the Sphinx or the pyramids.

Herodotus writes about a labyrinth above Lake Moeris, near the City of Crocodiles. The historian was taken through the huge buildings but was not permitted by the Egyptians in charge to see the basement halls. The refusal of the priests to show underground chambers to Herodotus is significant. Whether or not those subterranean halls contained historical records or tombs, is of secondary importance. The point we wish to prove is that Egypt did possess secret depositories.

The fraternity, which had reputedly saved papyri from the Alexandrian Library during the times of Cleopatra, may still be guarding a treasure in the valley of the Nile.

Freemasonry has preserved the tradition of secret vaults in its rites. The Rosicrucian Adepts have always been aware of the secret depositories of Egypt. In fact, the opening of the tomb of Christian Rosenkreuz, with its perpetual lamp, robot and secret manuscripts, is nothing else but the discovery of an ancient 'time capsule'. The Druce Masters of Lebanon have been custodians of their treasuries for hundreds of years.

Syria, now Lebanon, contains the ruins of Baalbek, a megalithic structure, the purpose of which may be identical with that of the Great Pyramid—to mark the site of an underground museum of a race which had existed before the Flood.

Josephus (first century) writes that the sons of Seth 'studiously turned their attention to the knowledge of the heavenly bodies and their configurations. And lest their science should at any time be lost among men, and what they had previously acquired should perish (inasmuch as Adam had acquainted them that a universal aphanism, or destruction of all things, would take place alternatively by the force of fire and the overwhelming powers of water), they erected two columns, the one of brick and the other of stone, and engraved upon each of them their discoveries."

The Jewish historian says that these inscriptions "remain even to the present day in the land of Syriad". This is a strong hint at pre-deluge records buried in Syria, possibly in Baalbek.

The huge foundation of Baalbek Terrace on which rest the Temple of the Sun, the Temple of Jupiter and several others, is completely out·of proportion to the size of the temples. Not much is left of the temple colonnades, yet the megalithic platform, upon which they stand, is still intact.

One stretch of that platform, composed of only three stones, is nearly 300 feet long. Some of the blocks weigh as much as 1,000 tons. The quarry is about a quarter of a mile away downhill. There lies a 70-foot long and 14 by 14 feet wide mass of stone as if left by the giants who had constructed the Baalbek.

How blocks of this size could have been raised from the quarry and delivered to the hill site, is a question which has remained unanswered for centuries. With all our supercranes, engineers of today would find it a difficult task to duplicate the effort of prehistoric builders of the terrace.

What is the aim of this cyclopean foundation? The Soviet

scientist M. M. Agrest advances a bold idea. What if under the colossal blocks of the Baalbek are hidden treasures for a mature mankind? What if under the shelter of megalithic rocks are located secret repositories of the space visitors? Dr M. M. Agrest thinks that when man understands the purpose of this monument of the Titans, he will receive a cultural inheritance from those who came to earth thousands of years ago.[61] The scientist's theory lends support to our basic theme of ancient repositories. The only difference is that we maintain the records were left by an advanced race of earth, who could have mastered space travel as well.

The American astronomer Frank Drake contends that the visitors from space could have left artifacts in limestone caves. These cosmic souvenirs might be tagged with radio-active isotopes whose artificial origin could easily be detected on our instruments. The caches were intended for an advanced terrestrial civilization in future ages. The time has come for their search.

SEEK IN THE MOUNTAINS AND THE SEA
Secret storehouses of a prehistoric civilization are located not only in the Mediterranean basin but also in other parts of the world.

For weeks I used to admire Kanchenjunga with its veil of snow, looming high above the horizon. Why is this Himalayan peak called the 'Five Sacred Treasures of the Great Snow?' Are treasures really buried deep within its bosom? Hillmen from Sikkim and Bhutan pay homage to the Five Treasures of Kanchenjunga. Tibetan folklore affirms that the precious things hidden in the innermost recesses of the mountain, have been guarded for centuries.

Nicholas Roerich, the famous painter and explorer, writes in *Himalayas, the Abode of Light* that the Himalayan foothills contain entrances to subterranean passages leading far below Kanchenjunga. He remarks that a closed stone door has been seen leading to the Five Treasuries of the Great Snow but the time is not ripe for its opening.

Also from Nicholas Roerich we learn that there are other secret storehouses in the Himalayas. On the Karakoram pass at an elevation of 19,500 feet, Roerich's groom said that great treasures were buried in the snowy ridge. He remarked that even the lowly ones among the natives knew of vast caverns which contained treasures from the beginning of the world. He wondered if Professor Roerich was aware of the books recording the location and contents of these subterranean vaults. The man of the mountains was asking Roerich why foreigners, who claimed to know so much, could not find the entryway to underground palaces. Then he concluded that the gates to them were guarded by a mighty fire which outsiders could not pass.[62]

These legends of hidden treasures are persistently heard in Asia. The Tibetan epic of Ghessar Khan predicts the opening of the Treasures of the Mountains.

India has a number of secret repositories according to H. P. Blavatsky. She wrote that initiated yogis knew of a vast network of underground galleries which run from cave temples. This engineering feat suggests a high technology in remotest antiquity.

In her travels through Tibet, Blavatsky met Buddhist pilgrims who claimed that in a secluded part of Altyn Tagh Ridge there existed a vast network of galleries and halls housing a collection of several million books. Madame Blavatsky estimated that the British Museum could not have accommodated all the cultural treasures of this underground library.[63]

The locality is described by her as a deep gorge with a small cluster of unimpressive houses to mark the site of what may be the world's greatest library. It is secure from intrusion and nothing will disturb its age-old manuscripts. The entrances are thoroughly concealed and the vaults with books lie deep within the bowels of the earth. It is most unlikely that our world will ever see this fabulous treasure-house of culture. But we can be more optimistic about the treasures of Atlantis buried in Egypt.

The sages of the East are in a position to present strange documents which will upset the opinions held by our historians. Blavatsky predicts that some of these manuscripts will soon be released.[64]

Our central topic of secret halls of records left by a former civilization may be hotly debated. Nevertheless, more significant than the writer's theories is the testimony given by Plato, Cicero, Manetho, Josephus, Proclus, Ibn Abd Hokm, Masoudi, and in recent times, by Blavatsky and Roerich.

The stage is now set for a momentous event in world history —the discovery of Atlantean antiquities. The prophetic words of Ignatius Donnelly, the American pioneer of Atlantology, uttered late in the last century, ring now in our ears: "Who shall say that one hundred years from now the great museums of the world may not be adorned with gems, statues, arms, and implements from Atlantis, while the libraries of the world shall contain translations of its inscriptions, throwing new light upon all the past history of the human race, and all the great problems which now perplex the thinkers of our day." [65]

'Time capsules' could also have been planted on the bed of the Atlantic when it was still dry land. These hermetically sealed vessels should contain a record of the accomplishments of Atlanteans in the realms of science and philosophy. A search for these capsules may reward the explorers with a priceless treasure.

Boris Liapunov, a distinguished Soviet writer who has given valuable help to the author in his work, has clear-cut ideas about Atlantis. In his book, *Ahead is the Ocean*, Liapunov writes:

Who can provide a definite solution in rejecting or vindicating Atlantis? Sea geologists and archaeologists. They will get the answer at the bottom of the ocean. Where exactly? Opinions are divided on that score. The name of Atlantis itself suggests the Atlantic Ocean. But the ocean is vast. Only an exploration of the relief of the bottom of the Atlantic will allow us to speak more or less definitely of the possible sites of the cataclysm. There are two prospects—the Azores and Canary Islands. In that area threatening volcanoes never stop to create and destroy land even in our own day.

The search is not going to be easy. The catastrophe took place a long time ago. It would be very difficult to discover its traces, covered with lava, ash and sediment, deep under the surface of the ocean. However, an advanced technology will come to our aid. Through the portholes of a bathyscape remnants of the Atlantis continent will appear to transform legend into fact.

Exploration of the Atlantic has already produced interesting evidence. Flying low over Bimini Islands an American pilot Robert Brush once spotted a strange square shape on the seabed which he photographed from the air. He showed the picture to French-born oceanographer Dimitri Rebikoff, who had spent twenty years in underwater exploration in the Mediterranean.

Rebikoff, president of the Institute of Underwater Technology, approached Dr J. Manson Valentine, a former Yale University professor, with a view to organizing an expedition to the site.

In 1968 they discovered that the dark rectangle on the seabed covered by 6 feet of water and overgrown with sea plants, was an ancient building, possibly a temple, approximately 100 by 75 feet in size. It is located near the north end of Andros Island, the largest island in the Bahamas.*

Anticipating disbelief from scientific quarters, Rebikoff remarked at the time that "Nature can make circular shapes and a lot of other shapes but nature cannot make a square angle —that is always the work of man."

And he added: "The archaeological rule is this—when you find a temple-like structure, there is a city or town around it. This is why we are optimistic about our discovery."

After examining the underwater ruins Dr J. Manson Valentine said: "What seems certain is that the ruin is pre-Columbus as established by its position relative to present water level."

The underwater explorer Dimitri Rebikoff who had surveyed more than a dozen sunken cities said: "I am as excited about this as about any of the Phoenician or Grecian explorations I have done."

* *The Miami News*, 23 August 1968. *The Miami Herald*, 11 September 1968.

Dr Valentine who had discovered many important Mayan relics in Yucatan, claimed that Rebikoff and himself had made out chambers or rooms in the ruins on the sea-bed. The fact that the building faced due east and west, and resembled the Uxmal Temple of the Turtles in Yucatan pointed at first to the Mayas as the builders. But when he considered that Rebikoff sighted in 1967 a quarter-of-a-mile-long rectangle from the air in the 3-fathoms-deep waters of the Great Bahama Bank, and that he himself had conducted aerial survey and photographed dozens of pathways with parallel sides, geometrical configurations and circular areas in the sea for 60 miles from Bimini to Orange Cay, their opinions began to change.

But more facts were necessary and these could only be obtained in further exploration. This is how J. Manson Valentine, Ph.D. described the discoveries: "But the most exciting piece of evidence that on a grand scale might indeed exist under the seas of our hemisphere came on the second day of September 1968, when the writer, diving in 3 fathoms off the north-west coast of North Bimini, was amazed to discern an extensive pavement of rectangular and polygonal flat stones of varying size and thickness, obviously shaped and accurately aligned to form a convincingly artifactual pattern. These stones had evidently lain submerged over a long span of time, for the edges of the biggest ones had become rounded off. Some were absolutely rectangular, sometimes approaching perfect squares. The larger pieces, at least 10 to 15 feet in length, often ran the width of parallel-sided avenues while the smaller ones formed mosaic-like pavements covering broader sections. Where the sand had washed away between them, another deeper layer of stones appeared below."

Dr Valentine admitted that it was difficult to ascribe an age to enigmatic pavements and stonework but he stated that they "might be as ancient as the legendary lands of Atlantis which were supposedly destroyed 11,500 years ago".

He believes that the Bahamas once harboured an advanced ancient civilization, because the Bimini builders were able to manipulate blocks as heavy as the ones employed in the construction of the Great Pyramid of Egypt or the stonework of

Cuzco in South America. "I've been in some kind of dispute with other scientists," said Dr Valentine with a smile. "I believe there was an Atlantis. I believe in it because of fact, because of various pieces of evidence that I have found in explorations in Yucatan, South America, Mexico and the West Indies."

Rebikoff shares his belief. "Atlantis is generally considered a myth but frequently archaeology has a way of proving out a myth. There is no good reason why we are not going to find sunken cities and buildings on the Bahama banks, based on what I've seen so far."

It may well be that an oceanographic probe will one day discover the lost Atlantean civilization.

But in the meantime indisputable evidence of a violent cataclysm in the Atlantic is already at our disposal. It does corroborate Plato's record of the sinking of Atlantis.

The 'Calypso' expedition of Jacques Cousteau discovered a huge grotto off the same island of Andros, with stalactites and stalagmites 165 feet under water. As these can only be formed in the air, the grotto must have been a cave well above sea level. From submarine sediments on the walls of the grotto it has been ascertained that the cave went down into the sea 12,000 years ago.

Cousteau's expedition also explored the 1,000-foot wide 'Blue Hole' off the coast of British Honduras. In the labyrinth of underwater caves the divers found slanted stalactites and stalagmites as if shaken by an earthquake. The analysis of one of these stalagmites conducted by scientists in Miami, showed that the deep grottos were above the Carribean 12,000 years ago.

It is apparent from these discoveries that violent geological upheavals occurred in the Atlantic basin about 10,000 B.C., the date of the proverbial 'Great Flood'.

Even before that time archaeologists can survey another field for possible antiquities from Atlantis—our museums. In the past certain objects could have been misclassified and their age underestimated. Articles identified as belonging to known cultures, may be actually of pre-deluge origin. This is an astounding possibility that can be exploited immediately.

The mysterious disc from Phaistos, Crete can be quoted as an example. It is a ceramic plate with strange pictographs arranged in a spiral. The hieroglyphics have not the slightest resemblance to the Linear A and B scripts of Crete. As the disc had been found in a Minoan palace together with a Linear A tablet, it was assumed to be of the same age, or 3,700 years old.

However, the clay from which the artifact is made, was not of Cretan origin. The pictographs were cast with wooden and metallic matrices. This *stamped* writing may thus be one of the earliest specimens of printing in the world.

It is rather curious that both the Denderah Zodiac of Egypt and the Baian-Kara-Ula discs of China contain picture-writing arranged spirally. There might be no connection at all between them if the text on the Phaistos disc, now in the Herakleion Museum of Crete, is eventually identified and decoded. But until then fantastic speculations about its antiquity and source can be advanced.

Artifacts of Atlantis may be hidden in grottos in the Andes or Himalayas. They may lie buried at the bottom of the Atlantic Ocean awaiting a bathyscaphe and television camera. Remnants of Atlantean culture may be stored under or in the pyramids to be discovered in a probe such as the one that the University of California and Ein Shams University of Cairo have been conducting.

They may be displayed with wrong labels at the Louvre, British Museum or elsewhere. Whether they are in museums, or the depths of the ocean or mountain caverns, the search for these objects should constitute the next target of science in an international programme of the exploration of time.

CHAPTER EIGHT

IT HAS ALL HAPPENED BEFORE

OUR DEBT TO ATLANTIS

Civilization is largely the product of human intelligence. From caves to skyscrapers, from boomerangs to space satellites, is a jump achieved by the power of mind. Deprive man of one half of his present intellect, and the whole social edifice of today will suffer a setback comparable with a planetary disaster. Culture the mind, and you will have a sky-rocketing civilization. Develop the moral nature of humanity, and you will have a utopia to live in.

Intellectual development in human society is not unlike a chain reaction in nuclear physics. Jean Sylvain Bailly, the French astronomer of the eighteenth century, summed up this process like this: "Ideas have been successively gathered together, heaped up; they have mutually engendered each other, the one has led to another. It remains therefore merely to rediscover this succession, to begin with the earliest ideas; the path is traced out; it is a journey that one may make again because it has already been made." [30]

Behind Copernicus, Galileo and Bruno stood the shades of Pythagoras, Aristarchus, Anaxagoras, Anaximenes and other Greek philosophers. Newton acknowledged his debt to antiquity by saying: "If I have seen further, it is by standing on the shoulders of giants."

But many of these giants of the classic world studied, in their turn, at the feet of Egyptian hierophants. From whom did the wise priests of the Land of the Nile receive their secret philosophic and scientific tradition? From Thoth, who had come from an island in the Western Sea. Thus the fount of learning can be traced to legendary Atlantis.

Much of the New World civilization is an enigma without the Atlantis theory. No race ever built such roads as the

Peruvians. They crossed the deepest canyons and pierced the highest mountains by tunnels which are still in use. On ancient asphalt-surfaced roadways modern cars travel today. No people, past or present, ever erected such megalithic structures as the pre-Incan races. No other nation ever has woven, by hand or machine, textiles of the workmanship of ancient Peruvians. No civilization ever had such an accurate astronomical calendar, in which every one of the 18,980 days were individually distinguishable, as the Aztecs and the Mayas.

Never in the world history till the twentieth century did any civilized nation live under any other economic system than that of private ownership. Yet the Incas had an economy in which money was non-existent. Everything belonged to the State. Regimented, perhaps, was the citizen of this South American empire, but he was secure in a welfare state built on strong ethical foundations.

When the white colonizers in Peru took over from the "Children of the Sun", they fitted doors with bolts and locks. The Quechua Indians were not slow in realizing that they had been conquered by thieves. They recalled the years under the Incas when doors had been kept open due to the absence of burglars.

In a planned economy agricultural projects seem to have been so effectively carried out that we owe to the pre-Incas and Incas half of the foods we eat today.

In the Old World ancient Greeks measured the width of the tropical zone and knew about the land of the midnight sun. They discussed the question of other habitable continents and even worlds in space. The Hellenes had enough of an idea of the solar system to make models of it and build planetariums.

The gap between rich knowledge and poor instruments in antiquity has baffled many a scientist. A present-day science writer in the U.S.S.R., Alexander Kazantsev, voices these reflections on the subject:

Amid the Egyptian pyramids, in the shadows of the columns in the temple of Ra, amid the white marble statues of Pallas and Jupiter, or in the philosophic solitude of the deserts, unknown scientists of remote antiquity perpetually observed the stars, laying foundation to astronomy—that science of nocturnal stillness, contemplative loneliness and sharp sight—the science of priests, dreamers and navigators, the science of exact calculations of time and space requiring complicated precision instruments. These were not available nor could they exist in ancient times, and yet certain astronomical knowledge of the ancients astounds us. Thousands of years before Copernicus and Galileo, the Egyptians knew well that the earth is a globe which revolves around the sun. Without any instrument for observation they were even aware how it moves. In ancient India the custodians of science—the priests—had long ago deduced that the universe was infinite filled with a multitude of worlds. It is inconceivable how the ancients knew of the earth's elliptical orbit round the sun. These 'flashes of learning' are in themselves of vast interest. The ancients were somehow in possession of the results of calculations rather than of the methods and equipment of precision instruments.[57]

A great portion of human progress can be attributed to evolution of society. However, some of the early achievements of mankind could have been a heritage from a prehistoric civilization.

Legends have faintly registered the voice of this vanished race. We must amplify it by means of deduction and imagination to make the voice clear and comprehensible.

Theory without factual corroboration leads to a labyrinth of speculation. On the other hand, the mere acquisition of facts degenerates into a data-collecting hobby. Each fact presented in this book may not be decisive in itself. It is only the correlation of all evidence that can bring the overall picture into focus.

When Columbus began his plans to cross the Atlantic in search of a westward route to India, he made a deep study of classic writers. There were numerous indications in their works that, contrary to the opinions of authorities, the earth was round. He concluded that, in theory, he could reach the East by sailing west.

At Lisbon he was shown puzzling wood water pipes brought by the Gulf Stream. Then news spread that two corpses of men with broad faces and black hair had been washed up at Madeira. They were smeared with strong essences which had protected the bodies from sharks and decomposition. The dead men were totally unlike any known people except Mongols. We now know that they were American Indians carried to Madeira from the Caribbean by the Gulf Stream. It was probably then that Christopher Columbus made his theory a working hypothesis.

The era of discovery and modern science began when progresssive intellectuals of the Renaissance turned their faces towards ancient Romans, Greeks and Egyptians to hear about a forgotten science and its benefits to humanity. This science of antiquity is the foundation upon which our contemporary civilization is built.

Our jet engine is but a perfected turbine invented by Heron of Alexandria. The slot-machine of today, which throws out chocolates and cigarettes, had a prototype in the temple of Zeus in Athens. It dispensed holy water, and the heavier the coin, the more water came out from the container. A thousand and one examples could be quoted to illustrate that there is nothing new except what has been forgotten.

We have travelled a serpentine road touching the lakes of fancy one moment and the rocks of fact the next. Closer and closer have we moved towards a view of an advanced race in the mists of the past which may have left a buried treasure for our science.

On these pages a controversy has been raised which nothing but Time can resolve, for has not Thales said that "Time is the wisest of things for it finds out everything"?

MAN IS ANCIENT

An overall picture of the expansion of human consciousness in the course of ages shows that man has lately begun to feel that the world is greater than it was thought a few centuries ago. Only in recent historical times did our ancestors discard the childish cosmology in which the earth was flat and the centre of the universe. In the past two hundred years science has proven that the cosmos is much vaster and older than our predecessors imagined.

If we approach the study of anthropology with a mind open to the possibility that man may be much more ancient than science holds, we will merely be detaching ourselves from the prejudices of the Middle Ages. Paleontology and archaeology have uncovered the remains of our primitive ancestors and their crude tools, and followed the human to his evolutionary infancy. Because the bones of Java, Peking and South Africa prehistoric men are the earliest found, it is supposed that *homo sapiens* appeared about one and a half million years ago. It is difficult to conceive cavemen leaving caves and trees a few thousand years ago and producing refined cultures of ancient Egyptians and Greeks in a few hundred generations. Though phenomenal accelerations are not foreign to evolution, it is essentially a very slow process.

It would be sheer obscurantism on our part to doubt the findings of science. The dating of prehistoric man, as we know him, is undoubtedly correct on the basis of evidence at our disposal at the present time. However, there is nothing impossible in discovering remains of older forebears of man. The greatest surprises may lie hidden in the sea-beds.

Archaeology considers the civilizations of Mohenjo-Daro, Sumer or Egypt as the earliest in history. In fact, science does not recognize any history as such prior to about 5000 B.C. Nevertheless, there may be relics of advanced nations buried in the oceans. If discoveries are ever made to that effect, history will have to make drastic corrections.

The rise of man from simple agricultural states of the valleys of the Nile, Tigris and Euphrates to our present technological era is too short a period for so fantastic an advance, unless man carried with him hereditary traits from another cycle of civilization.

To have progressed from ox-pulled carts to luxurious automobiles and from boomerangs to earth satellites in the short period of six thousand years is truly a miracle. But science has no place for miracles. Unknown factors could account for them. The time is too brief because it represents but a fraction of one per cent of the total accepted age of man. The "Caveman to spaceman in twenty-five thousand years" idea may be altogether erroneous.

It is anticipated that these views will be condemned by most scientists. Nevertheless, the controversy can be resolved overnight in our favour if one of the Atlantean 'time capsules' becomes accessible to the public. Until then the author is prepared to act as a target for the outbursts of irritated professors.

To summarize: man is more ancient than our academies conjecture. The earth has experienced violent cataclysms, mainly due to axis shifts and falls of huge meteorites. In these geological upheavals great civilizations disappeared without a trace.

Bhagavata Purana, a sacred book of India, speaks of four ages which have passed, each destroyed by the fury of the elements. Our present cycle is the fifth.

Hesiod, an ancient Greek poet who lived in the eighth century before our era, writes about a similar belief in Greece. There were four ages in the past. First, the gods created a golden race. They were mortal yet lived like gods. The second race was silver. They were of inferior intelligence. The next cycle was that of brass. Men were then strong and warlike and they destroyed themselves. The fourth era was the age of heroes whose adventures inspired men ever since. According to ancient Greek lore we are now in the fifth age—the age of iron. They believed we should likewise be destroyed by Zeus as were the other races. Censorinus (b. 238 A.D.) writes that the Greeks thought the world was either inundated or burnt after each epoch.

Ancient Egyptians divided history into three principal eras. First was the kingdom of the gods. In the second period demigods and heroes ruled on earth. Then with their departure, men reigned over Egypt and the world. When classic historians and myths speak of gods and demigods we do not take them seriously. Yet superior men could have walked the earth in a golden era.

In China the people of Yunnan have preserved the memory

of an age when levitation of heavy rocks was a commonplace matter, when all were prosperous and lived long lives. The Pai tribesmen sing of that bygone epoch in these words:

> In olden days rocks used to walk,
> Is this true or false?
> In olden days the rocks could walk,
> This is true not false.
> At that time the world was all peace,
> Do you believe what I say?
> At that time the world was all peace,
> I believe what you say.
> At that time there were no rich or poor,
> Do you believe what I say?
> At that time there were no rich or poor,
> I believe what you say.
> At that time people lived hundreds of years,
> Do you believe what I say?
> At that time people lived hundreds of years,
> I believe what you say.[66]

It is easy to call legends mere fantasy and laugh at the traditions of many peoples. It is much more difficult to appraise history in its entirety.

This work has an aim and a moral. Its aim is to call the attention of the public to the startling possibility of a discovery of a hidden depository left by a race now considered mythical. Its moral is contained in the question: "Are we not treading upon the footsteps of Atlantis?"

At the entrance of La Sainte Chapelle in Paris a guide was explaining to us the meaning of various ornaments. Before the panel depicting Noah's Ark and the Flood he delivered an oration on the biblical story of the Flood and concluded: "And so, *mesdames et messieurs*, people and animals began to multiply and, the process is still going on—till the next Flood."

According to Plato, the Atlanteans perished when they were engaged in imperialistic wars. But in a better epoch they loved peace, cherished camaraderie and despised avarice.

It is only hoped that the modern world may ensure a better destiny for itself than Atlantis. The Catalan poet Jacinto Verdaguer mourned Atlantis in these words:

> Atlantis, woe to thy children!
> Alas, shall we live to see another dawn?
> Our ancestor's words came true one by one:
> His Atlanteans, land and gods are no more.

Plutarch in *Isis and Osiris* recorded the opinion and belief of the most ancient sages "that there will become a fated and predestined time when the earth will be completely levelled, united and equal, there will be but one mode of life and but one form of government among mankind who will all speak one language and will live happily".

The discovery of the Treasure of the Ages will completely revolutionize all of our views on ancient history. From the lessons of the past, mankind will learn to avoid the mistakes of the vanished race. Man will then be able to find his proper place on this beautiful planet, his true mission and work towards a glorious future.

CHAPTER NINE

FROM LEGEND TO DISCOVERY

HISTORICAL PUZZLES

The story of a great civilization which sank under the waves of the Atlantic should not be regarded as something that does not concern us. If it is true, a similar geological catastrophe may one day befall our race. To think that the cities of today, teeming with life like anthills, could be submerged by oceans, is enough to make this myth more tangible.

The reality of Atlantis is abundantly attested by classic writers. For instance, Proclus (A.D. 412–89) states that: "The famous Atlantis no longer exists but we can hardly doubt but that it did once." The historian Strabo wrote in the first century before our era in reference to Poseidonius's works: "It is possible that the story about the island of Atlantis is not fiction."

Ours is not the first advanced civilization on earth, others may have preceded it. This is evident from folklore as well as history. Legend and myth, like strata of earth, provide an indication to historical events forgotten by man.

"It is not for me to say the last word. But I know that the time is near when this word will be said, and a colourful rainbow of conjectures rising over lost Atlantis will piece together into one picture Mayan ruins, Egyptian pyramids, the temples of India and legends of Oceania," once wrote K. Balmont, a poet of Russia.

The Greek myth of Deucalion and Pyrrha descending from Parnassus after the Flood, the only human beings in a dead world, is one of the numerous legends about the survivors of the last global disaster.

The *deus ex machina* (god from a machine) that brought ancient Greek dramas to a finale, could be a folk memory of an epoch when 'divine beings' had actually landed in flying machines to rehabilitate post-cataclysmic mankind.

"Thus in the beginning gods came to the earth often times; it was their sporting ground. But when the land became crowded with mortals, the visits of the immortals became few and far between. It was the privilege of some, however, to visit the immortals in heaven off and on for negotiations on behalf of mankind," writes Prof. H. L. Hariyappa in *Rigvedic Legends through the Ages*.

Is the legend of Daedalus and Icarus, who flew on wings from Crete, an echo of the dim past when aviation was commonplace?

The Aztec capital of Tenochtitlan was situated on an island in a lake, surrounded by concentric canals. It was so built because that was the plan of Aztlan in the east, from which the Aztecs claimed their descent. It could hardly be a coincidence that Tenochtitlan was almost a replica of the capital of Atlantis which Plato describes in the *Critias*.

In the old Chinese book of *Shu King* it is said that when the Emperor of Divine Dynasty saw no longer any trace of virtue in mankind, "he commanded Chong and Lee to cut away every communication between heaven and earth. Since then there has been no more going up and down". How can this passage be interpreted other than a record of air or space travel in prehistory?

The Indian Pantachantra contains a tale how once upon a time six youths constructed a dirigible airship, called 'Garuda', which could take off, land and fly in any direction. It was operated by an elaborate control system, producing even flight and perfect manoeuvring. One cannot but agree with Dr A. G. Bell, the inventor of the telephone, who said in 1907 that: "The old devices have been re-invented; the old experiments have been tried once more." Eighteen hundred years before Apollo 8 Lucian of Greece wrote in *Vera Historia* of a vessel which travelled to the moon. In another tale his hero flies among the stars, but his presumption angers the gods who put an end to the cosmic voyages of this early astronaut. Behind each myth lurks history. Is this ancient science fiction an expectation of a technology to come, or a recollection of a forgotten science?

Nearly two thousand years before Columbus stood disputing with the scholars and priests before Ferdinand and Isabella, there had lived men of science with a correct knowledge of the earth. Eratosthenes, in the third century before our era, held that "if the extent of the Alantic Ocean were not an obstacle, we might easily pass by sea from Iberia (Spain) to India." In the first century before our era Strabo also recorded this well-founded tradition, saying that "it is possible that in the temperate zone there may be two or even more habitable continents".

Chi Meng, a Chinese sage and a contemporary of Strabo, taught that the blue of the sky is merely an optical illusion. In his work *Hsuan Yeh* he wrote that the stars, the sun and the moon float in empty space. This concept is certainly closer to truth than the image of a 'firmament' and flat earth, which prevailed in the Dark Ages under pressure of religious dogma.

The ancient Greeks—Thales, Anaxagoras and Empedocles—considered that the moon was illuminated by the sun. Democritus averred that the shapes one sees on the moon are to be attributed to the heights of its mountains and the depths of its valleys. Fifteen hundred years passed and, thanks to prelates and frightened scholars, the moon turned into a celestial lantern of undetermined nature and size, kindly provided by God to dispel nocturnal darkness.

Helena Blavatsky summed up this decadence by saying that after Constantine: "The vista into the far distant past, beyond the Deluge and the Garden of Eden, began to be forcibly and relentlessly shut out by every fair and unfair means from the indiscreet gaze of posterity. Every issue was blocked up, every record upon which hands could be laid, destroyed." Alfred Dodd writes along the same lines in *Francis Bacon's Personal Life Story*: "Theology led men away from the great thinkers of Greece and Rome. Under the leadership of the priest, civilization plunged blindly forward into the abyss of the Medieval Era."

About a thousand years before that gloomy age Kanada, a thinker of India, advanced his atomic theory and, like a

134

twentieth-century scientist, concluded that light and heat are only different forms of the same basic substance.

Plutarch in his *Life of Lysander* writes that meteors are "a falling of celestial bodies, which in consequence of a certain intermission in the rotary force, have been hurled down". Hundreds of years later, at the opening of the nineteenth century, the Academy of France wrote a letter in regard to a fall of meteorites in Gascony, expressing regret "that in our enlightened age there can still be people so superstitious as to believe stones fall from the sky". Strange as it seems today, classic philosophers were more mature intellectually than our ancestors in the eighteenth century. Democritus is known to have laughed so hard at the follies of the world, some thought him mad. The man who said, "In reality there is nothing but atoms and space," had a perfect right to laugh at the ignorance of mankind.

Cicero writes in the *Commonwealth* that Marcus Marcellus possessed a 'celestial globe' from Syracuse, which demonstrated the motion of the sun, moon and planets. He assures his readers that the machine "was a very ancient invention". And yet we ourselves began to build such planetariums only in recent times.

In Australia aborigines have X-ray paintings in which animals, fishes and reptiles are masterfully shown with their internal organs and bones. Do the Australian aborigines possess X-ray vision, similar to the ability to sense colours blindfolded with one's fingers (extra-ocular vision) which is already recognized by science? Or are these unusual paintings a race memory of a bygone age when X-ray equipment was used? In fact, the aborigines have a name for that age—Dreamtime, a past so far away that it has lost its reality.

In one of the Buddhist Jatakas is mentioned a magic gem capable of raising into the air whoever holds it in his mouth. A Chinese alchemist Liu An, known as Huai-nan Tse, discovered an anti-gravity liquid in the second century before our era. He drank the elixir and was instantly raised into the air in broad daylight. When he dropped the bottle with this chemical solution into his courtyard, his dogs and poultry sipped the dregs and also became airborne. Let us not ridicule these curious tales because many fantasies of the Orient have become real through modern science.

The astronomers of antiquity were aware of the solar parallax, the apparent displacement of the sun's position due to the change in the observer's position. However, with the simple instruments then in use, they could not have arrived at it. The first observation of the sun's parallax was made in 1670 by William Gascoigne with a wire-netting placed across telescopic lens. But ancient astronomers did not have telescopes. How did they do it?

At the source of all ancient civilizations there always stands a divine bearer of culture. Thoth brought a ready-made culture from a western land. His titles 'Lord of the Overseas' and 'Guardian of the Two Lands' by which he is referred to in the Book of the Dead and certain Pharaonic inscriptions, suggest that he was an Atlantean leader. A significant myth about the god Thoth says that it was on wings that he transported the gods to the east—to "the other side of the lake Kha". Airlift of a cultural *élite* from Atlantis to Egypt?

The Chinese book *I-Ching* credits "celestial genii" with having introduced agriculture on earth for the benefit of the human race. Incidentally, the origin of maize is puzzling. Its fossils have never been found in a wild state. Its growth has been invariably connected with humans. It is old because traces of corn were detected in a geological stratum, corresponding to an epoch 30,000 years ago. Almost the same can be said in regard to wheat. Were the plants developed from primitive forms in early Atlantis, or imported from another planet as the Eastern tradition claims?

Australian tribes attribute their culture to sky-beings, such as Baiame, Daramulun and Bunjil. However, the natives admit that they know nothing about the history of these heavenly messengers before they arrived among them.

In the Museum of the American Indian, Heye Foundation, in New York, there is a large Maya jar of red pottery with a complex design. It has been ascertained that a pattern drawn on a flat surface was transferred on to the jar in three dimensions with an exactitude that few living draughtsmen could duplicate. This speaks for the presence of instruments and mathematics in Central America in a past epoch.

Iran traditions mention a gallery in the mountains of Khaf (Caucasus) with statues of the Wise Kings of the East whose lineage was thousands of years old. Taimuraz, the third king of Iran, visited this cave mausoleum on a winged steed, called Simorgh-Anke, which was born before the Deluge. This myth will become clear once it is assumed that Taimuraz had an airship of Atlantean origin in which he flew to the most ancient tombs of Khaf.

Legend has it that under the city of Cuzco, Peru, lie caverns with treasures. In the past centuries many adventurers tried to gain access to these vaults but none have returned. Finally, one man came back with two heavy golden bars but with his mind gone. It was then that the Peruvian government ordered the entrances walled up. On this subject American author L. Taylor Hansen wrote these lines in an article a number of years ago: "And would it be too much to hope, that when these vast caverns are in a future century revealed, perhaps to a more civilized world and a more cultured world than we have today, we may find not just goldbars, but the infinitely more precious libraries, which could have untangled what are today such a mass of snarled and conflicting legend?"

Oliva recorded a tradition told to him by an Indian quipu-reader that the real Tiahuanaco is a subterranean city. This legend may allude to underground vaults containing the cultural treasures of the Incas.

A similar tale was brought from Mexico by the Conquistadores. They write that, in spite of tortures, the Maya priests refused to reveal the location of the hidden fifty-two golden tablets on which was inscribed the ancient history of the New World.

According to Diogenes Laertius (third century) the archives of Egyptian priests were 49,500 years old in his day. Modern scientists will but smile at this claim of a high culture at a time when man is supposed to have been a savage. This raises a provoking question—is savagery in some instances the consequence of the fall of a high civilization, or merely the infancy of culture. Yucatan Mayas are in a primitive state today but their ancestors were once proud and wise. Their fall was caused by wars and colonialism. A terrestrial calamity with inundations and volcanic eruptions is able to reduce civilized men to savages. This is a theory which should be examined without any bias.

"All the issues connected with the sunken continents compel us to reappraise our views on the culture, way of life and traditions of those peoples which were formerly called 'primitive' or 'savage'. It appears that they are not the younger but the elder brothers of the human family," thus wrote I. Kolubovsky in the *Red Gazette* of Leningrad in 1927.

MYTHS PROVEN TRUE

The Mansi tribe in the Arctic tundra of Siberia has a legend. Long, long ago a firebird lived with the ancestors and it was so warm that giant trees grew and queer animals grazed. But someone stole the firebird and severe cold and winds set in. The strange trees and animals perished.

This is not a myth but a scientific fact as fossils of prehistoric trees and animals are found in Siberian tundra. Verbal accounts, handed down from generation to generation, can often preserve an amazing degree of accuracy.

We have talked a great deal about myths in this book. The average person thinks they are a by-product of fancy. However, this is not always the case. Folklore, as the collective memory of the human race, contains many records of past events, often coloured by ancient story-tellers and unavoidably distorted because of the passing of legends from one generation to another. But not unfrequently traditions are actual fossils of history. It is utterly unscientific to discard mythology as a collection of fables. A reality of yesterday, is a myth today. The world we live in, will be hardly more than a myth itself ten thousand years from now. In that distant future, sages will engage in polemics about the mythical character of legends connected with our vanished civilization.

Until about two hundred and fifty years ago the cities of Herculaneum and Pompeii were nothing but a myth. After their excavation and discovery the two cities became history. When I saw Pompeii, the city seemed to be only asleep.

Among the more fabulous stories of Herodotus is the tale of a distant country where griffins guard a golden treasure. Soviet archaeologists have discovered that country. It is Altai, or Kin Shan in Chinese, meaning the golden mountain. Gold mines have been located there since ancient times. In the valley of Pazyrka scientists have found remains of a high culture. Rich decorations prominently display the griffin. Thus a vague myth about griffins guarding the gold has ceased to be a mere legend.[67]

Although the mountain stronghold of Petra, lost in the desert south of the Dead Sea, was described by Eratosthenes, Pliny, Eusebius and others, in time it became a legendary city. It was only at the dawn of the nineteenth century that Burckhardt gained entrance into the gorge and beheld an edifice carved out of solid rock, an amphitheatre and numerous caves. Once again a fable was turned into fact.

When Heinrich Schliemann started excavations on the mounds of Hissarlik in Asia Minor in 1870 in search of the legendary city of Troy, professors thought he was mad. Yet the *Iliad* of Homer was right—Troy was no myth. Schliemann found ruins of a city which was even more ancient than Troy itself. Eventually Troy's remains were identified to the triumph of Heinrich Schliemann.

The story of Diego de Landa, written in 1566, about the Sacred Well of Sacrifice in Yucatan into which human victims and jewellery were thrown, has been regarded by historians as a mere tale. Then in the nineteenth century an American diplomat and archaeologist E. H. Thompson discovered the well of Cichen-Itza and validated the old Indian legends.

Six hundred years ago a Chinese ambassador, Chow-Ta-Kwan, submitted to his emperor a report of a fantastic walled city, the hub of a thriving kingdom, south of China, completely lost in the jungle. When the document was published in 1858, Western scholars dismissed it as fiction. Before long a French naturalist—A. H. Mouhot—stumbled upon the remains of Angkor Thom in Indo-China. The description of the legendary jungle city by the mandarin surprisingly corresponded to the actual panorama of Angkor Thom.[68]

When Marco Polo returned to Europe with tales of black

stones found in China which burned and heated daily baths, the Venetians of his day only laughed. First of all, no stones could burn, secondly how could anyone in the world afford such a luxury as a hot bath daily? The reader has, no doubt, recognized the reference to coal in Polo's story. His accounts of black oil of the Caspian available in large quantities from the bowels of the earth, were also ridiculed. What were amusing tales to the citizens of Venice, are now scientific facts familiar even to children.

At times it is difficult to ascertain where myth ceases and history commences, or where history ends and myth begins. There is a tendency in scientific circles nowadays to regard mythology and folklore as sources of history. Dr Carl Sagan, a prominent United States astrophysicist, has successfully proved this point by referring to the voyage of La Perouse to the north-west of America in 1786. The legends of Indians who saw the ships of the navigator, contain amazingly accurate details as to the actual appearance of the French fleet which had visited the lands of these tribes. This shows how an actual event can be preserved in the memory of the masses by verbal transmission from one generation to another.

Guatemala Indians have interesting legends which date to the sixteenth century. When miraculous appearances of gods and their way of life were closely examined by the University of Oklahoma, it became apparent that the mythological beings were none other than the Spanish invaders.

Allowance must be made for inaccuracies, distortions and exaggerations which creep into a tale transmitted through the centuries. None the less, it may contain a kernel of truth and a chronicle of life in bygone epochs. In this light, we should not cast aside legends speaking of a highly advanced civilization of the past which perished in a planetary catastrophe.

Present-day science is gradually reiterating the wisdom of the ages. Have we not proven the correctness of the formula of Democritus—"in reality there is nothing but atoms and space"?

The children of ancient Greece were taught that the earth was a globe floating in infinite space. Their teachers knew about the relative sizes of the sun and the moon, and their approximate distances from the earth. Philosophers delivered lectures in forums about the Milky Way as a conglomeration of stars, each a sun in itself. In colonnaded temples learned men in tunics and togas spoke of life on other planets.

Almost two thousand years later the schoolchildren of Europe were taught that the earth was flat, the centre of creation, and that the stars were holes in the firmament. What right have we then to look down upon the sages of the classic world who possessed more wisdom than the theologians of the Dark Ages?

The tradition of the ancients in regard to a treasure hidden thousands of years ago, is not a myth. If we but take it as a working hypothesis, a great discovery could be made in this century.

Its impact on our life may be stronger than imagined. Evidence of a sudden geological cataclysm that had destroyed Atlantis, will necessitate adjustment in a science which admits no abrupt catastrophes on a planetary scale. History, with so many missing chapters, will gain an undistorted picture of the story of mankind. Our sociology will find out what social and economic systems had existed in the pre-cataclysmic world, and how they had developed—a fact of utmost importance in the modern conflict of ideologies. Archaic instruments or machinery constructed on principles unknown to us, might set our science on a new track. The acquaintance with the beliefs of the vanished race will show the growth of human consciousness. The discovery of a new world in time can be equated with the discovery of an inhabited world in space— both can set mankind in upheaval.

Great revelations have been made by questioning the accepted opinions of the times. Roger Bacon has well diagnosed the causes of human error in his *Opus Majus*: "For every person, in whatever walk of life, both an application to study and in all forms of occupation, arrives at the same conclusion by the three worst arguments, namely, this is a pattern set by our elders, this is the custom, this is the popular belief: therefore it should be held."

Like our predecessors we still live in a mentally conditioned society in which every departure from the recognized mode of thinking is regarded as a revolt against the idols of the time. But thousands upon thousands of people nowadays are beginning to think for themselves on all subjects. To them this book will be more than fiction.

In this era of the advancement of science let us await the most revolutionary archaeological find of all ages—the Treasure of Atlantis.

CHAPTER TEN

AUTHORITIES, ANECDOTES AND ATLANTIS

The more critical amongst us often say—"We want more facts." But it should not be overlooked that the mere accumulation of facts is not sufficient. It can become a mere philately. What is needed is the correct valuation of data and the practical application of knowledge.

This book contains a number of theories. It has been suggested that Atlantis was destroyed in a global cataclysm. We have speculated that some philosophers and scientists, who did not agree with the warmongering rulers of Atlantis, withdrew into inaccessible parts of our earth to live in protective isolation.

When the elements calmed down after the planetary disaster, and the earth again began to bear plants and animals, 'demigods' appeared to rehabilitate the human race. It was the golden age of heroes and culture bearers. It was the time when gods walked the earth.

To prove the existence of an archaic civilization unknown to our history, we offered an array of facts hinting at a prehistoric science. Then on the basis of ancient history and mythology it was surmised that the Atlanteans had left secret underground museums and libraries before the world flood.

Despite all care, this work may not be free from minor errors. All of these will be forgiven if one of the antediluvian museums is actually found. It is not improbable that this century will see the discovery of a treasure vault of a lost race. Then our principal thesis of the existence of a high culture thousands of years ago, will be vindicated.

Until a theory is confirmed by absolute proof, it is the experts who decide its worth. However, have authorities been wrong? The roadway of past history is full of fragments from fallen idols.

There are many historical instances when truth was temporarily eclipsed by error to be realised centuries later. According to Diogenes Laertius, Bion of Abdera (third century B.C.) was cognisant of "countries where there was day for six months and night for six months". This ancient knowledge of the inclination of terrestrial axis which is responsible for seasons and climates, was forgotten when the Dark Ages set in. A work entitled *On the Heretical Doctrine of the Globular Form of the Earth* by Lactantius Firmianus (A.D. 260–340) was published about five hundred years after Bion of Abdera. It is typical of the decadence of knowledge which prevailed in the Middle Ages: "Is it possible than men can be so absurd as to believe that there are crops and the trees on the other side of the earth that hang downward, and that men have their feet higher than their heads?"

Though the present chapter is written 'down-under' and the author's "feet are higher than his head", he feels no inconveniences whatever, contrary to Lactantius's fears.

The most exalted authorities have been guilty of wrong thinking. An example of shaken authority can be seen in the history of the discovery of America. When Columbus was seeking funds for his epoch-making voyage, he encountered great opposition from contemporary scholars. In the words of his son Ferdinand: "Some argued in this way. In all the thousands of years since God created the world, those lands had remained unknown to innumerable learned men and experts in navigation: and it was most unlikely that the Admiral should know more than all other man, past and present." [12]

But Christopher Columbus did, and to him goes the credit for thinking independently from the men of his day and not sharing their fallacies.

To demonstrate that there is no such thing as infallibility and that authorities have been wrong in the past, let us turn to the time of Leonardo da Vinci. When the great Leonardo proposed his 'aerial carriage', the learned ones were sceptical. In a *Discourse on the Impossibility of Mechanical Flight* written by Tito Ticinelli in 1613 we find these arguments:

I have decided to proceed to the disproving of another widespread fallacy—to wit, the notion that in future centuries it will be possible for men to fly by mechanical means. Leonardo da Vinci would have us believe that, if this bundle of materials were assembled into a sort of aerial carriage, the man holding them (or, it may be, sheathing himself within them) will not descend to the ground, but will soar aloft. I am not an opinionated man, but I give it now as my opinion that no reader in his senses will accept this reasoning of Leonardo.

In this age of fast-flying jets we can only smile at the limited reasoning of poor Ticinelli.

When Galileo constructed his telescope and was probing the depths of the heavens, Francesco Sizzi, an astronomer of Florence, was invited to join the inventor in observing the satellites of Jupiter. The Florentine star-gazer refused to look through the telescope for the following reasons: "These satellites of Jupiter are invisible to the naked eye and therefore can exercise no influence on the earth, and therefore would be useless, and therefore do not exist." [69] Sizzi admitted he was afraid that his beautiful system of cosmogony would fall to the ground because of Galileo's discovery. What he actually meant was this: "One ugly fact can destroy a beautiful theory."

The Church shared Francesco Sizzi's sentiments and in 1615 Galileo Galilei was denounced to the Inquisition for the Copernican 'heresy'. In the judgment against him as recorded by the Congregation of the Index 1633, it is stated that: "To assert that the sun, immobile and without local movement, occupies the centre of the world is an absurd proposition, false in philosophy, and moreover, heretical, since it is contrary to the testimony of the Scriptures. It is equally absurd and false in philosophy to say that the earth is not immobile in the centre of the world, and this proposition, considered theologically, is at least an error of faith."

Like the Church in olden times our scientific hierarchy has pretended to be infallible. The scientist sometimes forgets that he can be wrong, too. When Bouilland demonstrated Edison's

145

phonograph before the Paris Academy of Sciences in 1878, Du Moncel, a distinguished scientist, accused him of ventriloquism. The academicians of France did not even want to hear Bouilland explain the mechanism of the newly-invented machine, but branded him and Edison as impostors.

Lavoisier, eighteenth-century pillar of science, 'proved' that meteorites did not exist by this simple formula: "It is impossible for stones to fall from the sky because there are no stones in the sky."

In a speech before the British Association in 1838 Dr Lardner declared: "Men might as well project a voyage to the moon as attempt to employ steam navigation across the stormy North Atlantic Ocean." With the luxurious liners crossing the Atlantic daily and rockets heading for the moon, scepticism of this sort can bring laughter now. Baron Georges Cuvier (1769–1832), one of the great French naturalists, once said that: "Prehistoric men, physically different from the men of today, have never existed on earth."

In 1875 the Director of the U.S. Patent Office resigned on the grounds that everything had already been invented and there was nothing else for him to do. This is a comic example of the limitation of the human mind.

When Don Marcellino de Sautuola, the discoverer of Altamira cave paintings in Spain, presented his findings to an international congress of archaeologists in Lisbon in 1880, the men of science charged him with forging these rock paintings. His arguments that no artist in Spain could have presented extinct animals in so realistic a manner, were of no avail. We now know how hopelessly wrong was the scientific congress.

A British physicist P. G. Tait (1831–1901) upon hearing about the invention of the telephone in America exclaimed: "It is all humbug, for such a discovery is impossible." Professor Simon Newcomb, a prominent American astronomer, dogmatically asserted in 1903 that heavier-than-air machines were an impossibility: "The demonstration that no possible combination of known substances, known forms of machinery and known forms of force, can be united in a practical machine by which men shall fly long distances through the air, seems to the writer as complete as it is possible for the demonstration of any physical fact to be."

Fortunately for posterity, the Wright Brothers did not take the scientist too seriously and soon after invented the aeroplane. It is truly incredible to find a Ticinelli at the opening of this twentieth century. Strange as it seems now, he was not the only one.

In 1926 Professor A. W. Bickerton stated that the idea of shooting at the moon was foolish and impossible. Apollo 8 proved his judgment faulty.

In 1935 F. R. Moulton, a noted American astronomer, wrote that there was not the slightest possibility of man travelling in outer space. Dr Richard van der Riet Wooley, formerly Astronomer Royal, obviously echoed Moulton's narrow scepticism when he remarked in January, 1957, that space travel was "utter bilge". Eight months later Sputnik I was orbiting the earth.

There were not too many scientists in the world until 1938 who could visualize a living coelacanth in the Indian Ocean. The reason was simple—the prehistoric fish had been considered dead for 75 million years. Yet this spectre of evolution was captured in 1938 and in 1952–1955, and studied by science.

In view of these historical anecdotes should we take all scientific scepticism seriously? One cannot help agreeing with Arthur C. Clarke, the British expert on the conquest of space, who has propounded the following law: "When a distinguished but elderly scientist states that something is possible, he is almost certainly right. When he states that something is impossible, he is very probably wrong." [70]

Our authorities have proven by their errors in the course of centuries that they are sometimes but the blind leading the blind.

The progress of science has been greatly hindered by a negative approach and an excess of conservatism where it is least needed—in new fields of research. Conservatism, as a chain to the past, is dialectically incompatible with movement into the future. Everything is possible in time and what is impossible today, will be a reality tomorrow. With a fiery dialectic of this kind, great discoveries will inevitably be made in the future.

In the meantime, the theory of Atlantean 'time capsules' will most likely be afforded the same treatment by contemporary scientists as evolution, the phonograph, telephone, aeroplane and space rocket received from their colleagues in the past.

In this epoch of a chain reaction in science man will acquire as much knowledge in the next fifteen years as he has from the beginning of history up to date. This is an estimation by Academician A. I. Berg of U.S.S.R.* Consequently, the Atlantis hypothesis could be vindicated long before the end of this century.

* Sovietskaya Russia, October 19, 1967.

SOURCES

Foreign languages: D—Dutch
                  F—French
                  G—German
                  P—Polish
                  R—Russian

1   R. D. M. Verbeek, *Krakatau*, Batavia, 1885.   D
2   E. Andreyeva, *In Search of a Lost World*; Detgiz, Leningrad, 1961.   R
3   *Priroda* (magazine), No. 7. 1955.   R
4   *San Francisco Examiner*, 14 July 1958.
5   N. F. Zhirov, *Atlantis*, Mysl, Moscow, 1964 and *Literatournaya Gazeta*, 23 November 1963.   R
6   Geological Society of America, Bulletins Nos. 60 (1949) and 65 (1954).
7   C. H. Hapgood, *Earth's Shifting Crust*, Pantheon Books, New York, 1958.
8   R. Altamira, *A History of Spain*, D. Van Nostrand Co. Inc., New York, 1952.
9   Smithsonian Institution, Bulletin No. 57 (1915), Washington, D.C.
10 *Technica Molodezhi*, Nos. 9–12, 1956.   R
11 C. W. Ceram, *Gods, Graves and Scholars*, Victor Gollancz Ltd., London, 1952.
12 F. Columbus, *The Life of the Admiral Christopher Columbus*, Rutgers University Press, New Brunswick, N.J., 1959.
13 L. Zajdler, *Atlantyda*, Wiedza Powszechna, Warsaw, 1963.   P
14 R. Robinson, *The Feathered Serpent*, Edwards and Shaw, Sydney, 1956.
15 H. P. Blavatsky, *The Secret Doctrine* (Vol. III), Adyar, Madras, 1938.
16 *Noir et Blanc* (magazine), Paris, 19–25 May 1966.
17 F. Soddy, *The Interpretation of Radium*, John Murray, London, 1909.
18 F. Ossendowski, *Beasts, Men and Gods*, E. P. Dutton & Co., 1926.

19 N. Roerich, *Gates into the Future*, Uguns, Riga, 1936.   R

20 N. Roerich, *Himalayas, Abode of Light*, Nolanda Publications, Bombay, 1947.

21 A. David-Neel, *The Superhuman Life of Gesar of Ling*, Rider and Co., London, 1959.

22 N. Roerich, *Heart of Asia*, Roerich Museum Press, New York, 1929.

23 A. Besant and C. W. Leadbeater, *Man: Whence, How and Whither*, Adyar, Madras, 1913.

24 Mahatma Letters, Rider and Co., London, 1948.

25 E. E. Clark, *Indian Legends of the Pacific Northwest*, University of California Press, 1953.

26 *Los Angeles Times*, 22 May 1932.

27 W. S. Cerve, *Lemuria*, AMORC, San Jose, California.

28 A. H. Verrill, *Old Civilizations of the New World*, The New Home Library, New York, 1943.

29 W. J. Perry, *The Children of the Sun*, Methuen and Co. Ltd., London, 1923.

30 J. S. Bailly, *Histoire de l'Astronomie Ancienne et Moderne*, Paris, 1781.   F

31 J. E. Gore, *Astronomical Essays*, Chatto and Windus, London, 1907.

32 K. K. Doberer, *The Goldmakers*, Nicholson and Watson, London, 1948.

33 W. R. Dawson, *The Frazer Lectures*, MacMillan & Co., Ltd., London, 1932.

34 *Smena* (magazine), No. 8, 1961.   R

35 *Smena* (magazine), No. 1, 1962.   R

36 *Discovery* (magazine), May 1963, London, and *Nature* (magazine), 11 November 1886, London.

37 *Natural History* (magazine), September 1955, U.S.A.

38 D. Saurat, *Atlantis and the Giants*, Faber and Faber, London.

39 P. Honore, *In Quest of the White God*, Hutchinsons, London, 1963.

40 *Science* (magazine), 6 November 1964, Washington, D.C.

41 *Atlantis* (bulletin), July–August 1966, 19 Berkley Street, London, S.W.1.

42 J. Alden Mason, *The Ancient Civilizations of Peru*, Penguin Books, 1957.

43 R. Charroux, *Histoire Inconnue des Hommes*, Robert Laffont, Paris, 1963.   F

44 B. Laufer, *Prehistory of Aviation*, Field Museum of Natural History, Chicago, 1928.

45   R. N. C. Bowen, *The Exploration of Time*, George Newnes Ltd.,
     London, 1958.
46   W. B. Carpenter, *The Microscope and Its Revelations*, J. and A.
     Churchill, London, 1891.
47   *Daily Mirror*, 9 January 1959, Sydney.
48   *Popular Electronics* (magazine), July, 1964, U.S.A., and W.
     König, *9 Jahre Irak*, Verlag Rudolf Rohrer, Baden bei Wien,
     1940.   G
49   C. N. Mehta, *The Flight of Hanuman to Lanka*, Narayan
     Niketan, Nodiad, Bombay, 1940.
50   I. Idriess, *Drums of Mer*, Angus and Robertson, Sydney, 1962.
51   Professor Dr Afetinan, *The Oldest Map of America*, Turk Tarih
     Kurumu Basimevi, Ankara, 1954.
52   *Sydney Morning Herald*, 15 September 1962, Sydney.
53   *China Pictorial* (magazine), No. 8, 1958.
54   *China Reconstructs* (magazine), August 1961.
55   J. C. Ferguson, *The Mythology of All Races* (Vol. VIII), Marshall
     Jones Co., Boston, 1928.
56   *Smena* (magazine), 29 September 1960.   R
57   A. Kazantsev, *Steps of the Future*, Gospolitizdat, Moscow,
     1963.   R
58   *Los Angeles Times*, 16 November 1962.
59   *Vestnik Znania* (magazine), Nos. 5–6. 1930.   R
60   M. P. Hall, *Masonic, Hermetic, Qabbalistic and Rosicrucian
     Symbolical Philosophy*. The Philosophical Research Society
     Press, Los Angeles, 1947.
61   M. Agrest, *On Land and at Sea*, Geografgiz, Moscow, 1961.   R
62   N. Roerich, *The Indestructable*, Uguns, Riga, 1936.   R
63   H. P. Blavatsky, *Secret Doctrine* (Vol. I), Adyar, Madras, 1938.
64   H. P. Blavatsky, *Secret Doctrine* (Vol. V), Adyar, Madras, 1938.
65   I. Donnelly, *Atlantis*, Sidgwick and Jackson, London, 1960.
66   *China Reconstructs* (magazine), December 1960 (Supplement
     "Creation").
67   P. M. Ouspensky and K. Schneider, *Behind the Seven Seals*,
     Molodaya Gvardia, Moscow, 1963.   R
68   P. E. Cleator, *The Past in Pieces*, George Allen and Unwin Ltd.,
     London, 1957.
69   M. Davidson, *The Stars and the Mind*, Watts and Co., London,
     1947.
70   A. C. Clarke, *Profiles of the Future*, Victor Gollancz Ltd.,
     London, 1962.

INDEX

155

A Selection of Popular Non-Fiction from Sphere

QUEEN ALEXANDRA	Georgina Battiscombe	75p
THE SUN KING (illus.)	Nancy Mitford	£1.00
THE PRINCE OF PLEASURE (illus.)	J. B. Priestley	£1.50
THE EDWARDIANS (illus.)	J. B. Priestley	£1.95
ELIZABETH I (illus.)	Neville Williams	£1.00
THE TOMB OF TUTANKHAMUN (illus.)	Howard Carter	£1.50
TUTANKHAMUN: THE LAST JOURNEY (illus.)	W. MacQuitty	75p
NOT OF THIS WORLD (illus.)	Peter Kolosimo	35p
GODS AND SPACEMEN IN THE ANCIENT EAST	W. Raymond Drake	35p
WE ARE NOT THE FIRST	Andrew Tomas	35p
INSIDE THE THIRD REICH	Albert Speer	75p
HITLER'S LAST DAYS	Gerhard Boldt	35p

A Selection of Science Fiction from Sphere

A Selection of Westerns from Sphere

Zane Grey

Frederick H. Christian

T. V. Olsen

A Selection of Crime Thrillers from Sphere

All Sphere Books are available at your bookshop or
newsagent, or can be ordered from the following address:

Sphere Books, Cash Sales Department,
P.O. Box 11, Falmouth, Cornwall.

Please send cheque or postal order (no currency), and allow
7p per copy to cover the cost of postage and packing
in U.K. or overseas.